Table Of Contents

Section 7: Troubleshooting and Support

Section 8: The Future of Automation in Smartsheet

Appendices

- **Appendix A**: Smartsheet Automation Templates and Checklists
- **Appendix B**: Glossary of Key Automation Terms
- **Appendix C**: Additional Resources and Learning Tools

~ Conclusion

Disclaimer

This book is an independent resource and is not officially affiliated with, endorsed by, or sponsored by any company, organization, or trademark holder referenced within. All trademarks, service marks, product names, and company names or logos mentioned are the property of their respective owners. Use of these names or terms is solely for identification and reference purposes, and no association or endorsement by the respective trademark holder is implied. The content of this book is based on publicly available information, the author's research, and personal insights. This book is intended for educational and informational purposes only.

Welcome & What You'll Learn

Welcome to The Ultimate Guide to Smartsheet Automation

In today's fast-paced work environment, efficiency and automation are no longer luxuries—they are necessities. Smartsheet has emerged as a powerful platform that enables teams to manage projects, collaborate seamlessly, and, most importantly, automate repetitive tasks to maximize productivity. This book is designed to guide you through the full spectrum of Smartsheet automation, from fundamental concepts to advanced integrations and real-world applications.

Whether you are a project manager looking to streamline workflows, a business leader seeking operational efficiency, or a team member aiming to reduce manual workload, this guide will provide you with actionable insights and best practices to harness the full potential of Smartsheet's automation capabilities.

Why This Book?

With the growing reliance on digital tools for work management, automation has become a game-changer for organizations of all sizes. However, understanding and implementing automation effectively requires more than just familiarity with the platform—it demands a strategic approach. This book will help you:

- **Understand the importance of automation** in modern workflows and how it enhances efficiency.
- **Navigate Smartsheet's automation features** and configure them to suit your needs.
- **Leverage core automation tools** such as alerts, approvals, task assignments, and data integrations.
- **Explore advanced automation techniques** that involve formulas, conditional logic, third-party integrations, and API-based custom solutions.
- **Apply automation to real-world scenarios** across industries, including project management, HR, marketing, operations, and finance.
- **Optimize and troubleshoot automations** to ensure reliability and effectiveness.

Who Should Read This Book?

This book is designed for professionals across various industries who want to enhance their productivity using Smartsheet automation. You'll benefit from this guide if you are:

- A **project manager** looking to automate task assignments, approvals, and reporting.
- A **business executive** aiming to improve workflow efficiency and data-driven decision-making.
- An **operations manager** seeking to reduce manual interventions in repetitive processes.
- A **team leader or coordinator** responsible for keeping projects on track with minimal effort.
- A **Smartsheet user** at any experience level who wants to harness automation to simplify work.

How This Book is Structured

This guide is divided into eight sections, each covering a crucial aspect of Smartsheet automation:

1. **Introduction to Smartsheet Automation** – Learn what automation is, why it matters, and how Smartsheet enables automated workflows.
2. **Getting Started with Smartsheet Automation** – Set up your account, understand automation permissions, and configure basic settings.
3. **Core Automation Features in Smartsheet** – Explore essential automation tools such as alerts, reminders, task assignments, and workflow automation.

4. **Advanced Automation Techniques** – Go beyond the basics with conditional logic, formulas, integrations with tools like Zapier, Microsoft Teams, Slack, and API-based custom solutions.
5. **Real-World Applications and Use Cases** – See how Smartsheet automation is used in project management, marketing, HR, finance, and customer service.
6. **Best Practices and Optimization** – Learn how to design efficient workflows, avoid common mistakes, measure automation success, and scale automation across teams.
7. **Troubleshooting and Support** – Resolve common errors, debug formulas, and leverage Smartsheet's support resources.
8. **The Future of Automation in Smartsheet** – Explore AI-driven trends, skill development, and emerging automation strategies.

Additionally, the **Appendices** provide valuable templates, a glossary of key terms, and additional learning resources to enhance your automation expertise.

How to Get the Most Out of This Book

To make the most of this guide, consider the following approach:

- **Follow the sections progressively** to build a strong foundation before diving into advanced techniques.
- **Apply what you learn in real time** by experimenting with Smartsheet's automation features alongside reading the book.
- **Use the real-world use cases** as inspiration to implement automation strategies tailored to your needs.
- **Refer to the appendices** for ready-to-use templates and additional learning resources.

Let's Begin!

By the time you finish this book, you will have a deep understanding of Smartsheet automation and be equipped with the knowledge to implement efficient, automated workflows in your organization. Let's embark on this journey to transform the way you work with Smartsheet!

Section 1:
Introduction to Smartsheet Automation

What is Automation?

Automation is the process of using technology to perform tasks with minimal human intervention. It involves the creation of workflows, scripts, or software-driven actions that replace repetitive, manual processes. By reducing manual effort, automation enhances efficiency, reduces errors, and allows teams to focus on high-value work.

In today's digital world, automation is a key driver of productivity across industries. Businesses use automation to streamline project management, data processing, customer communication, financial reporting, and much more. From simple rule-based tasks to advanced artificial intelligence (AI)-powered workflows, automation is transforming how work gets done.

Types of Automation

Automation can take many forms, depending on the complexity of the tasks and the level of human involvement. Here are some key types of automation:

1. Rule-Based Automation

This involves predefined rules and triggers to execute specific actions. Examples include:

- Sending automated email responses when a request is submitted.
- Moving tasks to the next stage in a workflow when conditions are met.

2. Workflow Automation

Workflow automation connects multiple tasks or processes in a structured sequence. For example:

- Approving expense reports based on predefined conditions.
- Assigning tasks to team members automatically based on workload or role.

3. Robotic Process Automation (RPA)

RPA involves the use of software bots to mimic human actions, such as data entry, invoice processing, or form filling.

4. AI and Machine Learning-Based Automation

Advanced automation powered by AI can analyze patterns, predict outcomes, and make intelligent decisions. Examples include chatbots, recommendation engines, and fraud detection systems.

The Role of Automation in Work Management

In a work management environment, automation simplifies administrative tasks, enhances collaboration, and improves data accuracy. Instead of spending time on repetitive tasks like manual approvals, notifications, and tracking updates, teams can automate these functions, allowing them to focus on strategic initiatives.

Key benefits of automation in work management include:

- **Time savings:** Reducing manual steps speeds up workflows.
- **Consistency and accuracy:** Automation eliminates human errors.
- **Improved collaboration:** Team members stay informed without manual follow-ups.
- **Scalability:** Automated processes can grow with an organization's needs.

The Evolution of Automation

Automation has evolved significantly over the years. Initially, it was limited to simple macros and scripts. Today, platforms like Smartsheet offer no-code/low-code automation tools that allow users to create powerful automated workflows without requiring programming skills.

As organizations continue to embrace digital transformation, automation will play an even more crucial role in enhancing productivity and innovation.

How Smartsheet Fits into the Automation Landscape

Smartsheet is a versatile work management platform that integrates automation into its core functionality. It allows users to create automated workflows that:

- Send alerts and reminders.
- Automate approvals and task assignments.
- Trigger actions based on data changes.
- Integrate with other tools for seamless collaboration.

By leveraging Smartsheet's automation features, teams can significantly reduce manual effort and improve overall efficiency. The upcoming chapters will explore how Smartsheet enables automation and how you can implement it effectively in your workflows.

The Importance of Automation in Modern Workflows

In today's fast-paced business environment, organizations face increasing pressure to operate efficiently while managing complex workflows. The rise of remote work, global collaboration, and digital transformation has made manual processes not only inefficient but also a potential barrier to growth.

Automation has emerged as a critical solution to these challenges, allowing businesses to optimize operations, reduce errors, and improve decision-making. By automating repetitive tasks, teams can focus on strategic work, leading to greater productivity and innovation.

Why Automation Matters

Automation is no longer a luxury—it is a necessity for organizations looking to stay competitive. Here's why automation is essential in modern workflows:

1. Increases Efficiency and Productivity

Manual processes slow down operations, leading to wasted time and resources. Automation accelerates workflow execution by eliminating redundant steps and ensuring that tasks are completed with minimal human intervention.

For example, instead of manually assigning tasks, an automated system can instantly route them to the appropriate team members based on predefined conditions. This allows employees to spend more time on critical thinking and decision-making rather than administrative work.

2. Reduces Human Error

Errors in data entry, approvals, and reporting can be costly. Whether it's a miscalculated budget or a missed deadline, human mistakes can lead to project delays, compliance issues, and financial losses.

Automation eliminates the risk of human error by enforcing standardized processes and ensuring data consistency. For example, automated workflows in Smartsheet can validate inputs, flag inconsistencies, and send alerts for missing information, reducing the likelihood of mistakes.

3. Enhances Collaboration and Communication

In modern work environments, teams often operate across multiple locations and time zones. Relying on manual communication methods, such as email chains or phone calls, can lead to miscommunication and workflow bottlenecks.

Automation bridges this gap by streamlining communication through real-time notifications, task assignments, and approvals. With tools like Smartsheet, team members receive automated updates on project progress, ensuring transparency and accountability.

4. Accelerates Decision-Making with Real-Time Data

Informed decision-making relies on access to accurate, up-to-date information. Traditional manual reporting methods often involve delays and outdated data.

Automation enables real-time data collection, aggregation, and analysis, allowing managers and executives to make faster, data-driven decisions. Automated dashboards and reports in Smartsheet provide instant visibility into key performance indicators (KPIs), project statuses, and resource utilization.

5. Supports Scalability and Growth

As businesses grow, manual processes become increasingly difficult to manage. Scaling operations efficiently requires workflows that can handle increased workloads without additional manual effort.

Automation allows organizations to scale without compromising efficiency. Whether it's managing customer inquiries, tracking inventory, or processing invoices, automated workflows ensure that operations remain seamless as the business expands.

6. Ensures Compliance and Standardization

Industries such as healthcare, finance, and manufacturing require strict adherence to regulatory guidelines. Manually tracking compliance requirements can be challenging and prone to oversight.

Automation enforces compliance by standardizing processes, maintaining audit trails, and ensuring that all necessary steps are followed. Smartsheet's automation capabilities, such as conditional approvals and audit logs, help businesses maintain regulatory compliance effortlessly.

Real-World Impact of Automation

Let's look at some real-world scenarios where automation makes a significant impact:

- **Project Management:** Automated task assignments, status updates, and milestone tracking improve project efficiency and reduce delays.
- **Human Resources:** Automating employee onboarding, time tracking, and leave approvals streamlines HR operations.
- **Marketing Campaigns:** Automated email sequences, social media scheduling, and lead tracking enhance marketing efficiency.
- **Finance and Accounting:** Automating invoice approvals, expense reporting, and budget tracking ensures financial accuracy.
- **Customer Service:** Automated ticketing systems, chatbot responses, and feedback collection improve customer experience.

The Future of Automation in Workflows

As technology advances, automation is becoming even more sophisticated with the integration of artificial intelligence (AI) and machine learning. Future trends include:

- **AI-driven automation** that predicts workflow bottlenecks and suggests process improvements.
- **Hyperautomation**, where multiple automation technologies work together for end-to-end process optimization.
- **Seamless integrations** between work management platforms and external tools for a unified digital workspace.

Conclusion

Automation is transforming the way businesses operate, enabling them to be more efficient, accurate, and scalable. By embracing automation, organizations can reduce manual workload, improve collaboration, and drive continuous improvement.

Overview of Smartsheet's Automation Capabilities

Smartsheet is a powerful work management platform that allows teams to collaborate, manage projects, and streamline workflows efficiently. One of its standout features is its automation capabilities, which help reduce manual tasks and improve operational efficiency. By leveraging Smartsheet automation, businesses can create dynamic workflows that automatically handle approvals, notifications, data movement, and more, without requiring users to intervene constantly.

This chapter provides an overview of Smartsheet's key automation capabilities, helping you understand how they can be applied to improve your workflow processes.

Key Features of Smartsheet Automation

Smartsheet offers a variety of automation tools designed to enhance productivity and eliminate repetitive work. These tools enable users to set up workflows that trigger specific actions based on predefined conditions. Here are the core automation capabilities available in Smartsheet:

1. Automated Alerts and Notifications

- Send real-time alerts via email, Smartsheet notifications, or third-party integrations when specific conditions are met.
- Notify team members about upcoming deadlines, project status updates, or changes to critical data fields.
- Reduce the risk of missing important tasks by automating reminders.

2. Approval Workflows

- Create approval workflows that automatically request approvals from managers or stakeholders.
- Route approval requests based on predefined rules, such as budget thresholds or project phases.
- Speed up decision-making by allowing users to approve or reject requests directly from their email or Smartsheet interface.

3. Recurring Tasks and Scheduled Actions

- Automate recurring tasks such as weekly reports, monthly status updates, or periodic check-ins.
- Schedule actions to take place at specific times, ensuring consistency in work execution.
- Reduce the need for manual task creation and tracking.

4. Automated Task Assignments

- Assign tasks to team members automatically based on workload, project stage, or custom rules.
- Ensure accountability by linking automation to project deadlines and dependencies.
- Streamline delegation by dynamically reassigning tasks when conditions change.

5. Conditional Logic-Based Automation

- Set up workflows that execute different actions based on specified conditions (e.g., "If Status = 'Completed,' then notify the manager").
- Customize processes with multi-step conditional logic for more sophisticated automation.
- Improve efficiency by automating decision-making processes within workflows.

6. Data Movement and Integration Automation

- Automatically move or copy rows from one Smartsheet to another based on specific triggers.
- Link Smartsheet automation with external apps such as Microsoft Teams, Slack, and Google Drive for seamless collaboration.

- Reduce data redundancy by syncing data across multiple sheets.

7. Form-Driven Automation

- Capture form submissions and trigger automatic actions such as task assignments or approval requests.
- Send instant confirmations or follow-ups based on form responses.
- Improve response times by routing submissions to the appropriate team members.

8. Automated Reporting and Summaries

- Generate and distribute reports automatically at scheduled intervals.
- Summarize key performance indicators (KPIs) and progress metrics without manual effort.
- Keep stakeholders informed by delivering reports directly to their inboxes.

9. Integration with Third-Party Automation Tools

- Extend automation capabilities by integrating Smartsheet with platforms like Zapier, Microsoft Power Automate, and Smartsheet's API.
- Automate cross-platform workflows that connect Smartsheet with CRMs, marketing tools, or enterprise resource planning (ERP) systems.
- Create a seamless digital workspace by linking Smartsheet with the broader tool ecosystem.

How Smartsheet's Automation Works

Smartsheet's automation system is built around a simple, intuitive workflow builder that allows users to create and customize automated workflows without needing advanced technical knowledge. The process involves three main components:

1. **Triggers** – Define the event that starts the automation (e.g., when a row is added, updated, or a specific condition is met).
2. **Conditions** – Apply filters or rules to determine whether the automation should proceed (e.g., "If Priority = 'High,' then send an alert").
3. **Actions** – Specify what should happen when the trigger and conditions are met (e.g., notify a user, update a field, move a row).

Smartsheet provides a visual workflow builder that makes it easy to configure these elements, ensuring that even non-technical users can create powerful automation without coding.

The Benefits of Using Smartsheet Automation

By leveraging Smartsheet's automation features, organizations can experience a range of benefits, including:

- **Increased Efficiency:** Automating repetitive tasks reduces manual work and speeds up processes.
- **Improved Accuracy:** Eliminating human errors ensures consistency in workflow execution.
- **Better Collaboration:** Automated notifications keep team members informed and engaged.
- **Scalability:** Smartsheet automation can grow with the organization, handling more complex workflows as needed.
- **Cost Savings:** Reducing manual work and improving efficiency can lead to significant cost savings over time.

Conclusion

Smartsheet's automation capabilities provide a powerful way to enhance productivity, streamline workflows, and optimize work management processes. Whether you're automating simple task reminders or complex multi-step workflows, Smartsheet offers a flexible and user-friendly solution.

Benefits of Automating with Smartsheet

Automation is revolutionizing the way teams work by eliminating repetitive tasks, reducing errors, and improving efficiency. Smartsheet, a powerful work management platform, offers robust automation features that enable businesses to streamline their workflows, enhance collaboration, and scale their operations effectively.

In this chapter, we'll explore the key benefits of automating workflows with Smartsheet, demonstrating how its automation capabilities can improve productivity, accuracy, and decision-making.

1. Increased Productivity and Efficiency

One of the most significant advantages of automation is the reduction of manual work. Instead of spending hours on repetitive administrative tasks, teams can focus on more strategic activities.

Smartsheet automation helps improve productivity by:

- Automatically assigning tasks based on predefined conditions.
- Sending notifications and reminders to ensure deadlines are met.
- Streamlining approval processes to reduce bottlenecks.

For example, rather than manually checking for task completions, managers can set up automated alerts to notify them when a project phase is completed, saving time and improving workflow efficiency.

2. Reduced Human Errors

Manual data entry, task tracking, and reporting are prone to errors, which can lead to costly mistakes. Smartsheet's automation capabilities help eliminate human errors by enforcing structured workflows and ensuring accuracy.

With Smartsheet automation, you can:

- Standardize data collection using forms and automated validations.
- Prevent miscommunication with real-time updates and status changes.
- Use conditional logic to automatically update fields based on specific criteria.

For instance, an automated workflow can check for missing data in a submission and alert users to correct errors before finalizing a report, ensuring data accuracy across projects.

3. Enhanced Collaboration and Communication

In many organizations, teams work across multiple locations, time zones, and departments. Without automation, project updates, approvals, and progress tracking can become chaotic. Smartsheet's automation streamlines collaboration by ensuring that the right information reaches the right people at the right time.

Key collaboration benefits include:

- Automated notifications keeping stakeholders informed about project updates.
- Workflow approvals that ensure seamless decision-making.
- Real-time status updates that keep everyone on the same page.

For example, if a task status changes to "Needs Approval," Smartsheet can instantly notify the appropriate manager, reducing unnecessary delays and improving project coordination.

4. Improved Decision-Making with Real-Time Insights

Automation allows teams to access real-time data without manually compiling reports. By setting up automated reporting and dashboard updates, decision-makers can make informed choices based on the latest project status and performance metrics.

Smartsheet automation helps with:

- Scheduling automated reports that provide real-time insights.
- Tracking key performance indicators (KPIs) through live dashboards.
- Consolidating data from multiple sources for more accurate decision-making.

For instance, a project manager can receive an automated weekly report summarizing project progress, helping them identify potential risks and make proactive adjustments.

5. Scalability and Flexibility

As businesses grow, managing workflows manually becomes increasingly challenging. Smartsheet automation allows organizations to scale operations efficiently by handling larger volumes of data, users, and processes without additional overhead.

Scalability benefits include:

- Automating recurring tasks across multiple teams and departments.
- Easily modifying workflows to adapt to changing business needs.
- Integrating Smartsheet automation with other business tools like Slack, Microsoft Teams, and Zapier.

For example, a company expanding its operations across multiple locations can use Smartsheet automation to standardize project tracking and reporting across teams, ensuring consistency and efficiency.

6. Cost Savings

Reducing manual tasks and improving efficiency directly leads to cost savings. Automation eliminates the need for additional administrative work, reduces labor costs, and minimizes the risk of costly mistakes.

Ways automation helps cut costs:

- Reducing the time spent on data entry and repetitive tasks.
- Minimizing errors that could lead to rework or compliance issues.
- Optimizing resource allocation by automating task assignments.

For instance, automating invoice approvals can significantly reduce processing time, freeing up finance teams to focus on higher-value tasks.

7. Ensuring Compliance and Security

Many industries require strict adherence to compliance and security protocols. Smartsheet automation helps businesses maintain compliance by enforcing standardized processes and maintaining audit trails.

Key compliance benefits include:

- Automatically logging all workflow actions for audit purposes.
- Enforcing security measures such as role-based permissions and access controls.
- Automating compliance-related reporting to meet regulatory requirements.

For example, in industries such as healthcare and finance, automated workflows can ensure that approvals follow predefined compliance guidelines, reducing the risk of non-compliance.

8. Seamless Integration with Other Tools

Smartsheet automation doesn't operate in isolation—it integrates with a wide range of business applications, allowing teams to build cohesive workflows across platforms. By connecting Smartsheet with tools like Microsoft Teams, Slack, and Google Drive, businesses can enhance collaboration and workflow efficiency.

Integration benefits include:

- Automating data synchronization between Smartsheet and external apps.
- Enhancing cross-platform collaboration with automated notifications.
- Streamlining complex workflows using integrations with Zapier and APIs.

For instance, an automated workflow can create a Microsoft Teams message whenever a new task is assigned in Smartsheet, ensuring team members are instantly informed.

Conclusion

Smartsheet automation provides significant benefits, from increasing productivity and reducing errors to enhancing collaboration and decision-making. By leveraging Smartsheet's automation features, organizations can streamline operations, improve efficiency, and scale their workflows effortlessly.

Section 2:
Getting Started with Smartsheet Automation

Setting Up Your Smartsheet Account for Automation

Before you can fully leverage the automation capabilities of Smartsheet, you need to set up your account properly. A well-configured Smartsheet account ensures seamless workflow automation, optimal performance, and secure collaboration. This chapter will guide you through the process of setting up your Smartsheet account for automation, including account creation, plan selection, user roles, and essential settings.

1. Creating a Smartsheet Account

If you don't already have a Smartsheet account, follow these steps to create one:

1. **Visit Smartsheet's website** ([www.smartsheet.com] (https://www.smartsheet.com)) and click on **Sign Up or Start Free Trial**.
2. **Choose your preferred sign-up method**, such as using an email address, Google account, or Microsoft account.
3. **Verify your email** by clicking the confirmation link sent to your inbox.
4. **Set up your account details**, including your name, organization, and industry.

Smartsheet offers a **30-day free trial**, allowing you to explore its automation features before committing to a paid plan.

2. Choosing the Right Smartsheet Plan

Smartsheet provides different subscription plans, each with varying levels of automation capabilities. Selecting the right plan is essential for maximizing your automation potential.

Plan	Automation Features
Free Plan	Basic sheets, limited sharing, no advanced automation.
Pro Plan	Alerts & notifications, basic automation.
Business Plan	Advanced workflows, conditional logic, integrations.
Enterprise Plan	Unlimited automation, API access, security & compliance tools.

For teams that heavily rely on automation, the **Business or Enterprise plan** is recommended, as these offer advanced workflow automation, approvals, and integrations with third-party tools.

3. Setting Up Your Workspace and Sheets

Once your account is created, follow these steps to structure your workspace for automation:

a) Creating a New Workspace

A workspace helps you organize multiple sheets and collaborate with team members.

1. Click **Workspaces** in the left-hand navigation menu.
2. Click **Create Workspace** and name it according to your project or department.
3. Add relevant sheets and templates for automation workflows.

b) Creating a Sheet for Automation

To automate tasks, you need a structured sheet.

1. Click **Create → Grid** to start a new sheet.
2. Define **columns and data types**, such as text, dates, checkboxes, and dropdowns.
3. Populate your sheet with sample data to test automation settings.

4. Configuring User Roles and Permissions

Automation workflows often require collaboration across teams. Assigning appropriate **permissions** ensures that automation functions correctly while maintaining security.

User Role Levels in Smartsheet

Role	Permissions
Owner	Full control, can create and manage automation.
Admin	Can create automation but cannot delete sheets.
Editor	Can edit sheet data but cannot modify automation settings.
Viewer	Read-only access, cannot trigger automation.

To **assign roles**:

1. Open your sheet and click **Share**.
2. Enter the user's email and select their role.
3. Click **Send Invitation**.

For automation workflows that require user approvals, ensure **admins and editors** have the necessary access to trigger and manage automation.

5. Enabling Automation Permissions

Smartsheet requires specific permissions for automation workflows to function correctly.

- Navigate to **Admin Center** (for Business & Enterprise plans).

- Go to **Security & Controls** and enable **Automation Permissions**.
- Set permissions to **Unrestricted** or **Limited** based on your security needs.

If automation involves **external users** (clients, vendors, or contractors), ensure they have appropriate access to avoid workflow failures.

---

6. Integrating Smartsheet with Third-Party Tools

To enhance automation, you may need to integrate Smartsheet with other platforms such as Microsoft Teams, Slack, or Zapier.

- **Zapier Integration**: Automate tasks between Smartsheet and 5,000+ apps.
- **Microsoft Teams**: Get real-time Smartsheet updates in Teams.
- **Google Drive/OneDrive**: Sync files and documents automatically.

To set up an integration:

1. Go to **Account Settings → Integrations**.
2. Select the tool you want to connect.
3. Follow the authentication steps to link accounts.

---

7. Testing Automation Workflows

Before rolling out automation to your team, perform test runs:

- **Create a test sheet** with sample data.
- **Set up a simple automation rule** (e.g., an alert when a due date is missed).
- **Trigger the automation** by modifying data in the sheet.
- **Check if notifications, approvals, or task assignments are working correctly**.

---

8. Setting Up Automation Logging and Monitoring

To track automation performance:

- Go to **Automation Logs** under **Sheet Properties**.
- Monitor failed automation runs and adjust settings as needed.
- Use Smartsheet's **Activity Log** to review automation history.

Conclusion

Setting up your Smartsheet account correctly is the first step toward maximizing automation efficiency. By selecting the right plan, structuring workspaces, assigning permissions, and integrating with external tools, you ensure a seamless automation experience.

Navigating the Smartsheet Interface

Before diving into automation in Smartsheet, it's essential to familiarize yourself with the platform's interface. Understanding where key features are located and how they function will help you set up and manage automation workflows more efficiently. This chapter provides a comprehensive guide to navigating the Smartsheet interface, ensuring that you can easily access the tools you need for automation.

1. Overview of the Smartsheet Interface

When you log in to Smartsheet, you'll encounter a well-structured interface designed for easy navigation. The main components include:

- **Home Screen** – A centralized dashboard that displays recent sheets, reports, and dashboards.
- **Left-Side Navigation Panel** – Provides quick access to Workspaces, Recents, Favorites, and Browse options.
- **Sheets and Workspaces** – Organize your data and collaborate with teams.
- **Toolbar** – Houses key functions such as filtering, sorting, and adding automation.
- **Grid View** – The default spreadsheet-like interface for working with data.
- **Card, Gantt, and Calendar Views** – Different ways to visualize and interact with your data.

2. The Home Screen and Navigation Panel

a) Home Screen

The **Home Screen** serves as the starting point when logging into Smartsheet. It provides quick access to your most recent and frequently used items. Key features include:

- **Recent Items:** Quickly open recently accessed sheets, reports, and dashboards.
- **Pinned Favorites:** Keep your most-used Smartsheet items at the top for easy access.
- **Workspaces Overview:** View and manage workspaces where automation workflows are stored.

b) Left-Side Navigation Panel

The navigation panel provides access to key Smartsheet components:

Feature	Function
Home	Returns to the main dashboard.
Browse	Displays all your sheets, workspaces, and reports.
Recents	Shows your recently opened Smartsheet files.
Favorites	Allows you to bookmark important sheets or dashboards.
Workspaces	Displays shared workspaces where you collaborate with teams.
Solution Center	Lets you create new sheets, reports, and dashboards.

To quickly access your automation-enabled sheets, **use the Favorites feature** to pin frequently used files.

---

3. Sheets, Reports, and Dashboards

a) Sheets

Sheets are where you store and manage your data. They function similarly to spreadsheets but offer enhanced features such as automation, dependencies, and collaboration tools.

Key elements within a Smartsheet sheet:

- **Columns and Rows:** Store data, similar to Excel.
- **Cell Linking:** Connect data across multiple sheets.
- **Attachments & Comments:** Add supporting documents and communicate within cells.
- **Automation Panel:** Configure workflow automation directly within the sheet.

b) Reports

Reports allow you to consolidate data from multiple sheets into a single view. This feature is helpful for tracking project progress, task completion, or budget updates.

Automation Tip: **Use scheduled reports to automatically send updates to stakeholders at defined intervals.**

c) Dashboards

Dashboards provide a visual representation of key data points using widgets. They help in tracking automation performance by displaying real-time metrics such as:

- Number of pending approvals.
- Task completion rates.
- Upcoming deadlines.

---

4. Toolbar and Sheet Controls

Smartsheet's **toolbar** sits at the top of your workspace and provides essential tools for managing your sheets:

Toolbar Feature	Function
Filter	Display specific rows based on set criteria.
Sort	Organize data in ascending or descending order.
Conditional Formatting	Highlight rows based on conditions.
Automation	Set up workflows, alerts, and reminders.
Dependencies	Establish task relationships in project management.
Share	Add collaborators and manage permissions.

Automation Tip: **The Automation button lets you create new automation workflows or modify existing ones directly from the sheet.**

---

5. Viewing Data: Grid, Card, Gantt, and Calendar Views

Smartsheet provides multiple viewing options to cater to different workflow needs:

a) Grid View (Default View)

- Functions like a spreadsheet.
- Best for entering and managing raw data.
- Ideal for setting up automation workflows.

b) Card View

- Displays data as cards, similar to a Kanban board.
- Useful for task management and agile workflows.
- Drag-and-drop functionality for reassigning tasks automatically.

c) Gantt View

- Provides a timeline-based project tracking system.
- Enables automation of task dependencies and critical paths.
- Best for managing long-term projects with milestones.

d) Calendar View

- Displays tasks with due dates in a calendar format.
- Helps in scheduling and managing recurring automation triggers.

Automation Tip: **Use Calendar View to automate reminders for approaching deadlines.**

---

6. Accessing Automation Features

Smartsheet's automation capabilities are embedded directly into its interface. To access them:

1. Open any Smartsheet sheet.
2. Click on the **Automation** button in the toolbar.
3. Select **Create Workflow** to build custom automation.
4. Choose a **Trigger Event** (e.g., when a new row is added).
5. Define **Actions** (e.g., sending an alert or moving a row).
6. Click **Save** to activate the automation.

---

7. Customizing Your Smartsheet Workspace for Automation

To improve efficiency, consider customizing your Smartsheet environment:

- **Organize sheets into folders** within a workspace for easy access.
- **Use color-coding and labels** to categorize automation workflows.
- **Enable notifications** to stay updated on automated changes.
- **Set up role-based permissions** to control who can modify automation rules.

Automation Tip: **Create a dedicated workspace for automation testing to experiment with workflows before applying them to live projects.**

Conclusion

Navigating the Smartsheet interface efficiently is essential for managing automation workflows. Understanding key elements such as sheets, reports, dashboards, and the automation panel will help you streamline processes and maximize productivity.

Understanding Automation Permissions and Roles

In Smartsheet, automation permissions and roles determine who can create, modify, and execute automation workflows. Ensuring proper access control is essential for maintaining security, preventing unauthorized modifications, and ensuring that workflows function correctly. This chapter will provide a detailed breakdown of user roles, permissions, and best practices for managing automation access effectively.

1. The Importance of Automation Permissions in Smartsheet

Permissions in Smartsheet govern how automation interacts with data, users, and workflows. Setting the correct permissions ensures:

- **Security:** Prevents unauthorized access or changes to automation workflows.
- **Efficiency:** Ensures the right team members can create and manage automation without bottlenecks.
- **Accountability:** Keeps track of who modifies workflows and triggers automation actions.
- **Compliance:** Maintains proper data governance and workflow integrity.

2. User Roles in Smartsheet

Smartsheet offers different user roles, each with specific permissions that impact automation capabilities. Understanding these roles is crucial when assigning responsibilities for workflow creation and execution.

Role	Permissions	Automation Capabilities
Owner	Full control over sheets, workspaces, and automation.	Can create, edit, and delete automation workflows.
Admin	Can manage sheets and workspaces but not delete them.	Can create and modify automation workflows.
Editor	Can edit sheet data but cannot modify settings.	Can trigger automation but cannot create or edit workflows.
Viewer	Read-only access to sheets and dashboards.	Cannot trigger or modify automation workflows.

3. Types of Automation Permissions

Automation workflows in Smartsheet function based on specific permission settings. The level of access assigned to a user determines their ability to interact with automated workflows.

a) Sheet Automation Permissions

Sheet permissions dictate how users interact with automation on a per-sheet basis.

- **Unrestricted Automation:** Allows automation to run regardless of user access.
- **Limited Automation:** Requires the workflow creator to have full access to all automation-triggered actions.
- **Strict Automation:** Only runs actions if all participants have the required permissions.

b) Automation Action Permissions

When designing automation workflows, some actions require additional permissions:

Automation Action	Required Permission
Sending notifications and alerts	Viewer or higher
Moving or copying rows	Editor or higher
Assigning tasks to users	Editor or higher
Approving or rejecting requests	Admin or higher
Modifying workflow logic	Owner or Admin

4. Assigning and Managing Permissions

To ensure proper automation functionality, you must configure access settings correctly. Follow these steps to manage user permissions effectively:

a) Assigning Permissions to Users

1. Open the **Smartsheet Sheet or Workspace** where automation is applied.
2. Click **Share** in the top-right corner.
3. Enter the email address of the user you want to add.
4. Select their **role (Owner, Admin, Editor, or Viewer)**.
5. Click **Send Invitation** to grant access.

b) Modifying Permissions for Automation

If automation workflows require permission changes:

1. Navigate to the **Automation Menu**.
2. Select the workflow you want to modify.
3. Click **Permissions Settings**.
4. Choose **Unrestricted, Limited, or Strict** depending on security needs.
5. Save the changes to apply new permission rules.

Automation Tip: **For workflows requiring approvals or task assignments, ensure the users involved have at least Editor permissions to avoid automation failures.**

5. Common Automation Permission Issues and Solutions

Issue 1: Automation Fails Due to Insufficient Permissions

- **Cause:** Users triggering automation don't have the necessary access rights.
- **Solution:** Change the user's role to Editor or higher for automation to execute properly.

Issue 2: Users Cannot Modify Automation Workflows

- **Cause:** The user is assigned a Viewer or Editor role instead of Admin.
- **Solution:** Assign Admin or Owner roles to allow automation management.

Issue 3: Automated Row Movement Fails

- **Cause:** The user lacks permissions to modify the destination sheet.
- **Solution:** Ensure the user has Editor or Admin access to both the source and destination sheets.

---

6. Best Practices for Managing Automation Permissions

To ensure automation workflows function smoothly while maintaining security, follow these best practices:

a) Use Role-Based Access Control (RBAC)

- Assign permissions based on job function (e.g., Admins manage workflows, Editors update data, Viewers review reports).

b) Enable Logging and Audit Trails

- Track automation activity using Smartsheet's **Activity Log** to monitor changes and troubleshoot issues.

c) Restrict Automation Ownership to Key Users

- Limit the number of Admins and Owners who can modify critical automation workflows.

d) Test Permissions Before Deployment

- Run automation workflows in a test environment to verify that all users have the required access levels.

e) Regularly Review and Update Permissions

- Conduct periodic access audits to remove inactive users or adjust permissions as needed.

Conclusion

Understanding automation permissions and roles in Smartsheet is essential for creating secure and efficient workflows. By assigning the right user roles, managing automation settings, and following best practices, you can ensure that automation enhances productivity without compromising security.

Configuring Basic Automation Settings

Before implementing automation workflows in Smartsheet, it's essential to configure the basic settings to ensure seamless execution. Proper setup minimizes errors, enhances efficiency, and allows automation to run smoothly across your team or organization.

This chapter will guide you through the fundamental automation settings in Smartsheet, including workflow creation, trigger selection, action configuration, and best practices for automation setup.

1. Understanding Smartsheet Automation Workflows

Automation in Smartsheet operates through **workflows**, which consist of:

- **Triggers:** Define when the automation should run (e.g., when a row is added or updated).
- **Conditions:** Set specific criteria that must be met for the automation to execute.
- **Actions:** Specify what should happen once the conditions are met (e.g., sending an alert, moving a row, or updating a field).

To access automation settings:

1. Open a **Smartsheet sheet** where you want to configure automation.
2. Click the **Automation** button in the top menu bar.
3. Select **Create Workflow** to begin setting up your automation.

2. Configuring Triggers: When Automation Starts

Triggers determine when an automation workflow is activated. Smartsheet provides several trigger options:

a) Change-Based Triggers

These triggers activate when specific changes occur in a sheet.

- **When rows are added:** Executes automation when a new row is inserted.
- **When rows are changed:** Runs automation when a cell is updated (e.g., status changes from "In Progress" to "Completed").
- **When rows are deleted:** Activates automation when a row is removed.

b) Time-Based Triggers

These triggers execute automation at scheduled intervals.

- **Hourly, daily, or weekly automation** for regular updates or recurring reports.
- **Specific date triggers** to initiate actions on a particular day.

c) Recurring Triggers

These triggers help with periodic tasks, such as:

- Sending reminders before due dates.
- Generating weekly reports automatically.

Example: Setting a Change-Based Trigger

If you want to send an alert when a project status changes to "Completed":

1. Select **Trigger → When a row is changed**.
2. Choose the **"Status" column** as the monitored field.
3. Set the condition to **"When status changes to Completed"**.

---

3. Configuring Conditions: Refining Automation Execution

Conditions define when an automation should proceed. These filters ensure that workflows only execute when specific criteria are met.

a) Common Condition Types

- **If a specific column contains a value** (e.g., if "Priority" is "High").
- **If multiple conditions are met** (e.g., "Project Status = Pending" AND "Due Date is within 3 days").
- **If the assigned user matches a particular role** (e.g., only notify the project manager).

Example: Adding a Condition

If you want to notify only project managers when a high-priority task is assigned:

1. Add a condition: **"If Priority = High"**.
2. Set another condition: **"If Assigned To = Project Manager"**.

---

4. Configuring Actions: What the Automation Will Do

Once a trigger occurs and conditions are met, Smartsheet executes a predefined action.

a) Types of Automation Actions

Action	Purpose	Example
Send Alerts & Notifications	Notifies users about status updates.	Alert a manager when a task is overdue.
Request Approvals	Sends an approval request to a stakeholder.	Ask HR to approve an employee leave request.
Move or Copy Rows	Transfers data between sheets automatically.	Move completed tasks to an archive sheet.
Update Cells	Modifies cell values based on conditions.	Mark an order as "Shipped" when tracking details are added.

Example: Setting an Action

To send an alert when a task is assigned:

1. Select **Action → Send an alert**.
2. Choose **"Assigned To"** as the recipient.
3. Customize the alert message (e.g., "A new task has been assigned to you").

---

5. Testing and Activating Your Automation

Before rolling out automation across teams, test it to ensure it works as intended.

a) Steps to Test Automation

1. Create a test sheet with sample data.
2. Set up the automation with sample triggers and conditions.
3. Trigger an action (e.g., update a task status).
4. Verify that the automation executed correctly (e.g., did the assigned user receive a notification?).

Once verified:

- Click **Save and Enable Workflow** to activate automation.
- Monitor workflow execution under **Automation Logs**.

6. Managing and Modifying Automation Settings

After setting up automation, you may need to adjust settings based on workflow changes.

a) Editing an Existing Automation Workflow

1. Open your Smartsheet sheet.
2. Click **Automation → Manage Workflows**.
3. Select the workflow you want to edit.
4. Modify triggers, conditions, or actions as needed.

b) Disabling or Deleting Automation

If an automation workflow is no longer needed:

- Click **Disable Workflow** to turn it off temporarily.
- Click **Delete Workflow** to remove it permanently.

Automation Tip: **Regularly review automation settings to ensure they align with current business needs.**

7. Best Practices for Basic Automation Configuration

To maximize efficiency and avoid common pitfalls, follow these best practices:

- **Use clear and specific conditions** to avoid unnecessary automation triggers.
- **Set up alerts only when necessary** to prevent notification overload.
- **Test automation in a sandbox environment** before deploying it organization-wide.
- **Document your automation workflows** for future reference and troubleshooting.
- **Assign appropriate permissions** to prevent unauthorized users from modifying automation settings.

Conclusion

Configuring basic automation settings in Smartsheet is the first step toward streamlining workflows and reducing manual tasks. By properly setting up triggers, conditions, and actions, you can create automation workflows that enhance productivity and efficiency.

Section 3:
Core Automation Features in Smartsheet

Creating Automated Alerts and Reminders

Effective communication is essential for keeping projects on track, ensuring task completion, and maintaining workflow efficiency. In Smartsheet, automated alerts and reminders help teams stay informed without relying on manual updates.

By setting up automated notifications, you can reduce the risk of missed deadlines, improve collaboration, and enhance accountability. This chapter will guide you through the process of creating and configuring alerts and reminders in Smartsheet.

1. Understanding Automated Alerts and Reminders

Smartsheet provides two key notification automation types:

- **Alerts:** Instant notifications triggered by changes in a sheet (e.g., when a task is marked as completed).
- **Reminders:** Scheduled notifications that alert users about upcoming deadlines or tasks that require action.

Both alerts and reminders ensure that stakeholders receive timely updates based on pre-set conditions, reducing the need for manual follow-ups.

2. How to Create Automated Alerts

Alerts notify users when specific actions occur in a Smartsheet sheet. They can be sent via email, mobile notifications, or integrations with tools like Slack or Microsoft Teams.

Steps to Create an Alert in Smartsheet

1. **Open the Smartsheet Sheet** where you want to configure alerts.
2. Click on the **Automation** button in the top menu.
3. Select **Create Workflow → Alert Someone**.
4. Choose a **Trigger** (e.g., "When a row is added" or "When a row is changed").
5. Define **Conditions** (optional) to refine when the alert is sent.
6. Select **Recipients** (specific users, contacts in a column, or external stakeholders).
7. Customize the **Alert Message** to include relevant details.
8. Click **Save** and activate the workflow.

Example Use Case: Alerting a Manager When a Task Is Completed

- Trigger: When a row is changed.
- Condition: If "Status" = "Completed".
- Action: Send an alert to the assigned manager.

This ensures that managers are automatically notified as soon as a task reaches completion.

3. How to Create Automated Reminders

Reminders ensure that users are notified before a deadline or task due date, helping prevent missed deadlines.

Steps to Create a Reminder in Smartsheet

1. Open the **Automation Menu** and select **Create Workflow**.
2. Choose **Set a Reminder** as the workflow type.
3. Select a **Trigger** (e.g., "When a date is reached").
4. Set the **Timing** of the reminder (e.g., "1 day before the due date").
5. Choose the **Recipients** (team members, project managers, or external users).
6. Customize the **Reminder Message** to include task details.
7. Click **Save** and enable the workflow.

Example Use Case: Reminding Employees About an Upcoming Deadline

- Trigger: When the due date is approaching.
- Timing: 2 days before the due date.
- Action: Send a reminder to the assigned employee.

This setup ensures that employees receive timely notifications and stay on top of their assigned tasks.

4. Customizing Alerts and Reminders

Smartsheet allows you to customize alerts and reminders to improve clarity and relevance.

a) Personalizing Messages

- Include the task name, due date, or status update in the message.
- Add action steps for recipients (e.g., "Please review and approve this task.").

b) Choosing the Right Notification Method

- **Email:** Best for formal communication.
- **Mobile Notifications:** Ideal for on-the-go updates.
- **Slack/Microsoft Teams Integration:** Useful for teams using collaboration tools.

c) Setting Up Conditional Alerts

- **Example:** Only notify the finance department if an expense exceeds $1,000.
- **How?** Use **"If column contains X"** conditions to refine notifications.

5. Managing and Modifying Alerts and Reminders

After setting up alerts and reminders, you may need to modify them based on project changes.

a) Editing an Existing Alert or Reminder

1. Open the **Automation Menu** in Smartsheet.
2. Click on **Manage Workflows**.
3. Select the workflow you want to modify.
4. Adjust the trigger, conditions, or recipients as needed.

5. Click **Save** to apply changes.

b) Disabling or Deleting an Alert

- To disable an alert temporarily, toggle the **Off/On** switch in the automation settings.
- To delete an alert permanently, select **Delete Workflow** from the options menu.

Automation Tip: **Regularly review alerts and reminders to ensure they are still relevant and necessary.**

---

6. Best Practices for Using Automated Alerts and Reminders

To maximize efficiency and avoid notification overload, follow these best practices:

- **Set alerts only for critical updates** to prevent unnecessary distractions.
- **Use reminders sparingly** to avoid overwhelming users with excessive notifications.
- **Ensure messages are clear and actionable** so recipients understand what needs to be done.
- **Combine alerts with approval workflows** to streamline decision-making.
- **Test alerts and reminders before deployment** to verify accuracy.

Conclusion

Automated alerts and reminders in Smartsheet improve communication, reduce manual follow-ups, and help teams stay on track with their tasks. By configuring triggers, conditions, and actions effectively, you can ensure timely updates and prevent missed deadlines.

Setting Up Recurring Tasks and Approvals

Many business processes involve repetitive tasks and approvals, such as weekly status updates, monthly financial reviews, and project milestone approvals. Manually managing these tasks can be time-consuming and prone to errors. Smartsheet's automation features allow you to set up recurring tasks and approvals to streamline workflow execution, improve accountability, and ensure consistency.

This chapter will guide you through setting up automated recurring tasks and approval workflows in Smartsheet to reduce manual work and improve operational efficiency.

1. Understanding Recurring Tasks and Approvals in Smartsheet

Smartsheet's automation engine allows users to:

- **Schedule recurring tasks** that repeat on a daily, weekly, or monthly basis.
- **Set up automatic approvals** that route requests to the appropriate stakeholders.
- **Ensure accountability** by tracking approvals and due dates.

By implementing these features, teams can improve efficiency and avoid missing critical deadlines.

2. Setting Up Recurring Tasks in Smartsheet

A recurring task is any task that needs to be completed on a regular basis. Instead of manually entering the same task each time, you can automate its creation using Smartsheet workflows.

Steps to Automate Recurring Tasks

1. **Open Your Smartsheet Sheet**
   - Navigate to the sheet where tasks are tracked.
2. **Click on the Automation Button**
   - Select **Create Workflow → Record a Date**.
3. **Choose a Recurring Trigger**
   - Select **When a Date is Reached** as the trigger.
   - Define the recurrence frequency (daily, weekly, monthly, or annually).
4. **Define the Task Details**
   - Set columns such as **Task Name, Due Date, Assigned To, and Status**.
   - Use the **Modify Row** action to update existing rows instead of creating new ones.
5. **Save and Enable the Workflow**
   - Click **Save** to activate the recurring task automation.

Example: Automating a Weekly Project Status Update

- **Trigger:** When the due date is reached.
- **Frequency:** Every Monday at 9 AM.
- **Action:** Create a new row with "Weekly Status Update" and assign it to the project lead.

This setup ensures that every Monday, a new task is created for project managers to submit their status updates.

3. Setting Up Automated Approvals in Smartsheet

Automated approvals help streamline decision-making processes by routing requests to the appropriate stakeholders. Approvals can be used for:

- Expense approvals.
- Time-off requests.
- Purchase order authorizations.
- Project milestone sign-offs.

Steps to Automate an Approval Workflow

1. **Open the Smartsheet Sheet**
   - Use a sheet where requests and approvals are tracked (e.g., an expense approval sheet).
2. **Click on the Automation Button**
   - Select **Create Workflow → Request an Approval**.
3. **Define the Trigger**
   - Choose **When a Row is Added** or **When a Row Changes**.
   - Example: If an expense report is submitted, the automation is triggered.
4. **Add Conditions (Optional)**
   - Specify conditions to route approvals based on values in the sheet.
   - Example: If "Amount > $1,000," send the request to a senior manager.
5. **Set Up the Approval Action**
   - Select **Request an Approval** as the action.
   - Choose the approver (a specific user or a contact listed in the sheet).
   - Customize the approval message (e.g., "Please review this expense request.").
6. **Define Actions Based on Approval Outcome**
   - If **Approved**, mark the request as "Approved" and notify the requestor.
   - If **Declined**, update the status to "Rejected" and notify the submitter.
7. **Save and Enable the Workflow**
   - Click **Save** to activate the approval automation.

Example: Automating an Expense Approval Workflow

- **Trigger:** When a new expense report is submitted.
- **Condition:** If the amount is greater than $1,000, send it to the finance team.
- **Action:** Send an approval request to the finance manager.

This ensures that high-value expense requests are reviewed and approved efficiently without requiring manual intervention.

---

4. Customizing Recurring Tasks and Approvals

Smartsheet allows for customization of recurring task and approval workflows to suit different business needs.

a) Using Conditional Logic for Approvals

- Example: If an expense is under $500, auto-approve it; if it's over $500, route it for manager approval.
- Set up conditions in the **If/Then** logic to define multiple approval paths.

b) Assigning Approvers Dynamically

- Instead of a fixed approver, Smartsheet allows dynamic approvals based on a column in the sheet (e.g., "Department Manager").
- This ensures approvals go to the right stakeholder based on the request type.

c) Integrating Notifications for Reminders

- Set up reminders for approvers if they have not responded within a set timeframe.
- Example: If no action is taken within 3 days, send a reminder email.

---

5. Managing and Modifying Recurring Tasks and Approvals

To modify or troubleshoot automation workflows:

1. **Access the Automation Menu**
   - Open the **Automation → Manage Workflows** tab.
2. **Edit Existing Workflows**
   - Modify triggers, conditions, or actions to reflect process changes.
3. **Disable or Delete Workflows**
   - Turn off automations that are no longer needed.
4. **Monitor Automation Logs**
   - Track failed automation attempts and adjust settings as required.

---

6. Best Practices for Automating Recurring Tasks and Approvals

To ensure automation is effective, follow these best practices:

- **Use clear and specific triggers** to avoid unnecessary automation runs.
- **Test workflows before deployment** to ensure tasks and approvals execute correctly.
- **Regularly review workflows** to adjust for changes in business processes.
- **Assign the right permissions** to prevent unauthorized modifications.
- **Notify stakeholders** to ensure they are aware of automated approvals and scheduled tasks.

Conclusion

Automating recurring tasks and approvals in Smartsheet significantly improves workflow efficiency, reduces manual workload, and ensures timely decision-making. By setting up scheduled task creation and automated approvals, teams can focus on high-value work instead of repetitive administrative tasks.

Automating Task Assignments and Notifications

Managing tasks efficiently is crucial for keeping projects on track and ensuring accountability within a team. Assigning tasks manually can be time-consuming, and without timely notifications, important updates may be overlooked.

Smartsheet's automation capabilities allow you to:

- Automatically assign tasks to team members based on specific conditions.
- Send real-time notifications to keep everyone informed.
- Improve collaboration by ensuring that task owners receive updates at the right time.

This chapter will guide you through setting up automated task assignments and notifications in Smartsheet to streamline workflows and enhance team efficiency.

1. Understanding Task Assignment and Notification Automation

Task assignment automation ensures that when a new task is added or updated in a sheet, the right team member is automatically assigned. This reduces manual work and prevents delays.

Notifications are used to alert users when:

- A new task is assigned to them.
- A task's status changes (e.g., from "In Progress" to "Completed").
- A deadline is approaching.

Combining automated task assignments with notifications creates a seamless workflow, ensuring that all stakeholders are informed in real-time.

2. Setting Up Automated Task Assignments in Smartsheet

Automating task assignments ensures that work is automatically allocated to the right individuals based on predefined criteria, such as task type, priority, or department.

Steps to Automate Task Assignments

1. **Open Your Smartsheet Sheet**
   - Navigate to the sheet where tasks are managed.
2. **Click on the Automation Button**
   - Select **Create Workflow** → **Assign a Task**.
3. **Choose a Trigger Condition**
   - Select when the automation should assign a task, such as:
     - "When a row is added" (new task creation).
     - "When a specific column changes" (task status updates).
4. **Set the Assignment Rules**
   - Select the **"Assigned To"** column.
   - Define assignment criteria (e.g., if "Task Type" is "Marketing," assign to the Marketing Manager).
5. **Enable Dynamic Assignments**
   - Instead of selecting a fixed user, use a column in the sheet that contains team members' names or email addresses.
6. **Save and Activate the Workflow**

    ○ Click **Save** to enable automatic task assignments.

- **Trigger:** When a new row is added.
- **Condition:** If the "Task Type" is "IT Support," assign it to the IT Manager.
- **Action:** Automatically set "Assigned To" as the IT Manager's email.

This setup ensures that new tasks are assigned to the right department or individual without manual intervention.

---

3. Setting Up Automated Notifications in Smartsheet

Once a task is assigned, automated notifications keep team members informed about updates, deadlines, and changes.

Steps to Automate Notifications

1. **Open the Smartsheet Sheet**
   - Ensure that an "Assigned To" column exists in the sheet.
2. **Click on the Automation Button**
   - Select **Create Workflow** → **Send an Alert**.
3. **Choose a Trigger Event**
   - Common triggers include:
     - When a row is added (new task assigned).
     - When a row is changed (task status updated).
     - When a due date is approaching.
4. **Set the Notification Conditions**
   - Example conditions:
     - If "Status" changes to "Completed," notify the project manager.
     - If "Priority" is "High," notify the team immediately.
5. **Select Notification Recipients**
   - Send notifications to:
     - Specific users (managers, stakeholders).
     - The contact listed in the "Assigned To" column (dynamic notification).
6. **Customize the Notification Message**
   - Include details such as task name, due date, and action required.
7. **Save and Enable the Workflow**
   - Click **Save** to activate real-time notifications.

- **Trigger:** When a new task is created.
- **Action:** Send an email notification to the assigned user.
- **Message:** "A new task has been assigned to you: [Task Name]. Please review and update the status."

This ensures that team members are immediately informed when a task is assigned to them.

---

4. Customizing Task Assignments and Notifications

Smartsheet allows customization of automation workflows to improve relevance and efficiency.

a) Using Conditional Logic for Assignments

- Example: Assign tasks to different team members based on project priority.
- How? Use **"If Priority = High, assign to Senior Manager"** logic in the workflow.

b) Assigning Tasks to Multiple Users

- Example: If a task requires multiple people, set the "Assigned To" column as a multi-contact field.
- How? Enable multiple contacts in the column settings before automation setup.

c) Configuring Escalation Rules

- Example: If a task remains incomplete for more than 3 days, notify a senior manager.
- How? Add a time-based trigger to send notifications when a deadline is overdue.

---

5. Managing and Modifying Task Assignment and Notification Automation

After setting up automation, you may need to make adjustments as workflows evolve.

a) Editing an Existing Workflow

1. Open the **Automation Menu**.
2. Click on **Manage Workflows**.
3. Select the workflow you want to update.
4. Modify triggers, conditions, or recipients.
5. Click **Save** to apply changes.

b) Disabling or Deleting an Automation Workflow

- Toggle the **On/Off** switch to disable a workflow.
- Select **Delete Workflow** if the automation is no longer needed.

Automation Tip: **Regularly review and update automation settings to align with team structures and project changes.**

---

6. Best Practices for Automating Task Assignments and Notifications

To maximize efficiency and prevent notification overload, follow these best practices:

- **Use role-based assignments** to dynamically assign tasks to the right team members.
- **Limit unnecessary notifications** by refining trigger conditions.
- **Test workflows before full deployment** to ensure accuracy.
- **Set up escalation alerts** for overdue or stalled tasks.
- **Combine notifications with approval processes** for a seamless workflow.

Conclusion

Automating task assignments and notifications in Smartsheet helps streamline project workflows, improve collaboration, and ensure that team members stay informed about their responsibilities. By leveraging triggers, conditions, and dynamic notifications, teams can reduce manual work and improve efficiency.

Using Workflow Automation for Project Management

Effective project management requires coordination across teams, clear task assignments, and timely updates to keep everything on track. Manually tracking project progress can lead to missed deadlines, communication gaps, and inefficiencies.

Smartsheet's workflow automation streamlines project management by:

- Automating task assignments and approvals.
- Sending timely alerts and reminders.
- Managing dependencies and deadlines.
- Generating real-time progress reports.

In this chapter, you will learn how to leverage Smartsheet's workflow automation to improve efficiency, maintain project visibility, and ensure seamless collaboration.

1. Understanding Workflow Automation in Project Management

Project management workflows involve multiple steps, stakeholders, and dependencies. Smartsheet's automation capabilities help reduce manual effort by triggering actions based on predefined rules.

Common automated workflows in project management include:

- Task creation and assignment.
- Progress tracking and status updates.
- Automated approvals and stakeholder reviews.
- Deadline reminders and escalation alerts.
- Data synchronization and reporting.

By automating these tasks, project managers can focus on high-level strategy rather than administrative work.

2. Setting Up an Automated Project Workflow in Smartsheet

A well-structured workflow ensures that tasks move efficiently from one phase to another. Below is a step-by-step guide to setting up a project workflow in Smartsheet.

Step 1: Create a Project Sheet

1. Open Smartsheet and click **Create → Project Sheet**.
2. Set up key columns, such as:
   - **Task Name**
   - **Assigned To**
   - **Status** (e.g., Not Started, In Progress, Completed)
   - **Start Date & Due Date**
   - **Priority**
   - **Dependencies**

Step 2: Automate Task Assignments

To ensure tasks are assigned dynamically:

1. Click **Automation → Create Workflow → Assign a Task**.
2. Set a trigger, such as "When a row is added" (new task creation).
3. Define conditions, e.g., "If Task Type = 'Marketing', assign to the Marketing Manager."
4. Choose the **Assigned To** column as the recipient.
5. Save and activate the automation.

Example: Automatically Assigning Tasks to Teams

- **Trigger:** When a new row is added.
- **Condition:** If "Department" = "IT," assign to the IT lead.
- **Action:** Update the "Assigned To" column with the IT lead's email.

This automation ensures tasks are assigned without manual intervention.

---

3. Automating Progress Tracking and Status Updates

Tracking project progress requires constant updates. Smartsheet can automatically update task statuses based on conditions.

Steps to Automate Status Updates

1. Click **Automation → Create Workflow → Change a Cell Value**.
2. Set a trigger, such as "When a task is marked as complete."
3. Define an action, e.g., "Change Status to 'Completed'."
4. Save and enable the workflow.

Example: Automatically Updating Task Status

- **Trigger:** When "% Complete" reaches 100%.
- **Action:** Change "Status" to "Completed."

This prevents users from manually updating task statuses, reducing errors.

---

4. Setting Up Automated Approvals

Project approvals, such as budget sign-offs and milestone reviews, can be automated to reduce bottlenecks.

Steps to Create an Approval Workflow

1. Click **Automation → Create Workflow → Request an Approval**.
2. Set a trigger, such as "When a task reaches a specific stage."
3. Define the approver (e.g., project manager, client).
4. Customize the approval message.
5. Set an automatic action based on the approval outcome:
   - **If approved:** Move to the next phase.
   - **If declined:** Notify the submitter for revisions.

Example: Automating a Budget Approval Process

- **Trigger:** When a budget request is submitted.
- **Approver:** Finance Manager.
- **Action:** If approved, update "Approval Status" to "Approved."

This speeds up decision-making and reduces manual follow-ups.

---

5. Automating Deadline Reminders and Escalations

Project managers need timely alerts about approaching deadlines. Smartsheet can send reminders and escalate overdue tasks automatically.

Steps to Set Up Deadline Alerts

1. Click **Automation** → **Create Workflow** → **Send a Reminder**.
2. Set a trigger, such as "When a due date is approaching."
3. Define conditions, e.g., "If Status ≠ Completed, send a reminder 2 days before the due date."
4. Select the recipient (task owner, project manager).
5. Save and enable the workflow.

Example: Escalating Overdue Tasks

- **Trigger:** When a task is overdue.
- **Condition:** If "Status" is NOT "Completed."
- **Action:** Notify the project lead and escalate to senior management.

This automation ensures that no deadlines are missed.

---

6. Generating Real-Time Project Reports with Automation

Project managers often need up-to-date reports to track performance. Smartsheet can automatically generate and distribute reports.

Steps to Automate Project Reports

1. Click **Automation** → **Create Workflow** → **Send a Report**.
2. Select **Frequency** (daily, weekly, monthly).
3. Choose the report format (summary, detailed).
4. Set recipients (team members, stakeholders).
5. Save and schedule the automation.

Example: Weekly Project Summary Report

- **Trigger:** Every Monday at 9 AM.
- **Report Type:** Summary of pending and completed tasks.
- **Recipients:** Project team and executives.

This ensures project visibility without requiring manual report generation.

---

7. Managing and Modifying Project Automation

As project needs evolve, workflows should be reviewed and adjusted.

Editing an Automation Workflow

1. Open **Automation Menu** → **Manage Workflows**.
2. Select the workflow to modify.
3. Update triggers, conditions, or actions.

4. Save changes.

Disabling or Deleting Automation

- Toggle workflows **On/Off** as needed.
- Delete outdated automations to avoid clutter.

Automation Tip: **Regularly review and optimize workflows to ensure they align with project goals.**

---

8. Best Practices for Automating Project Management in Smartsheet

To maximize efficiency, follow these best practices:

- **Use dynamic task assignments** to automatically allocate work based on criteria.
- **Limit notification overload** by refining alert conditions.
- **Test workflows before full deployment** to prevent errors.
- **Combine automation with dashboards** for real-time project tracking.
- **Regularly update automation rules** to match project changes.

Conclusion

Automating project management workflows in Smartsheet improves efficiency, reduces manual work, and enhances team collaboration. By leveraging task automation, approval processes, deadline reminders, and reporting automation, project managers can maintain better control over project execution.

Automating Data Capture with Forms

Data collection is a critical process for businesses, but manual data entry can be time-consuming and error-prone. Smartsheet Forms provide a seamless way to automate data capture, ensuring that information is collected in a structured and organized manner. By integrating forms with Smartsheet automation, teams can eliminate manual input, trigger workflows, and streamline data processing.

In this chapter, we will explore how to create, customize, and automate Smartsheet Forms to optimize data capture for various business needs.

1. Understanding Smartsheet Forms

Smartsheet Forms allow users to submit structured information directly into a sheet without needing to manually enter data into a grid. Forms are ideal for:

- **Employee onboarding forms**
- **Customer feedback collection**
- **Project request submissions**
- **Expense reporting**
- **Incident tracking**

By automating data collection, organizations can ensure accuracy, improve efficiency, and trigger automated workflows based on form responses.

2. Creating a Smartsheet Form for Data Capture

Step 1: Open a Smartsheet Sheet

1. Navigate to the Smartsheet where you want to collect form responses.
2. Ensure the sheet includes the necessary columns for capturing the required data.

Step 2: Generate a Form

1. Click **Forms** in the top navigation menu.
2. Select **Create Form** to generate a new data entry form.

Step 3: Customize Form Fields

1. **Drag and drop fields** from the sheet to the form.
2. Adjust settings such as required fields, default values, and dropdown options.
3. Use **Conditional Logic** to show or hide fields based on user responses.

Step 4: Configure Form Submission Settings

1. Enable **Auto-Numbering** to track unique submissions.
2. Toggle **Allow Attachments** to let users upload documents.
3. Select **Restrict Access** if only specific users should submit responses.

Step 5: Share the Form

- Copy and share the **Form Link** via email or embed it on a website.
- Use **QR Codes** for easy mobile access.

3. Automating Workflows Based on Form Submissions

Once a form is set up, automation workflows can trigger specific actions whenever new data is submitted.

Example Use Case: Automating Employee Onboarding Requests

1. A new employee submits a form with their personal and department details.
2. Smartsheet automatically assigns IT, HR, and the hiring manager tasks.
3. A notification is sent to the HR team confirming the onboarding request.
4. The request is marked "Completed" once all steps are finalized.

Steps to Automate Workflows After Form Submission

1. Click **Automation → Create Workflow → Trigger Workflow on Form Submission**.
2. Choose a trigger condition:
    ○ **When a new row is added** (a form entry is submitted).
    ○ **When a specific column changes** (e.g., form response meets certain criteria).
3. Set an action, such as:
    ○ Assigning a task based on form data.
    ○ Sending an approval request.
    ○ Moving the row to another sheet.

Example: Automatically Assigning a Request Based on Department

- **Trigger:** When a new request is submitted via the form.
- **Condition:** If "Department" = "IT," assign the request to the IT Manager.
- **Action:** Update the "Assigned To" column with the IT Manager's email.

---

4. Automating Notifications for Form Responses

To ensure timely responses, automated notifications can be triggered when a new form submission is received.

Steps to Send Notifications on Form Submissions

1. Click **Automation → Create Workflow → Send an Alert**.
2. Set the trigger as **When a new row is added**.
3. Choose notification recipients:
    ○ Specific team members.
    ○ The user listed in the "Assigned To" column.
4. Customize the message to include submission details.
5. Click **Save** to activate the notification workflow.

Example: Notifying HR When a Job Application is Submitted

- **Trigger:** When a form entry is added to the "Job Applications" sheet.
- **Action:** Send an email to HR with the candidate's details.

---

5. Generating Reports from Form Data

Smartsheet allows you to generate automated reports and dashboards based on form submissions.

Steps to Create a Form Submission Report

1. Click **Create Report** → **New Row Report**.
2. Select the form's Smartsheet as the data source.
3. Apply filters to view submissions based on date, department, or status.
4. Enable **Scheduled Delivery** to send reports to stakeholders regularly.

Example: Weekly Summary of Customer Feedback Forms

- **Trigger:** Every Monday at 9 AM.
- **Report Type:** Summary of all customer feedback submissions.
- **Recipients:** Customer service and product development teams.

---

6. Best Practices for Automating Data Capture with Forms

To maximize efficiency, follow these best practices:

- **Use clear and concise form labels** to avoid confusion.
- **Enable required fields** to ensure users provide essential information.
- **Incorporate conditional logic** to streamline form complexity.
- **Set up automated approvals** for requests that require review.
- **Regularly review and optimize automation settings** to ensure workflows stay relevant.

Conclusion

Automating data capture with Smartsheet Forms simplifies information collection, enhances accuracy, and reduces manual work. By integrating forms with workflow automation, businesses can streamline operations, improve response times, and ensure that collected data is used effectively.

Streamlining Reporting with Scheduled Summaries

In any organization, reporting is essential for tracking progress, analyzing data, and making informed decisions. However, manually compiling reports can be time-consuming and prone to errors. Smartsheet's **Scheduled Summaries** feature automates reporting, ensuring that key stakeholders receive up-to-date insights without requiring manual intervention.

By leveraging **automated reporting**, you can:

- Generate and distribute reports on a predefined schedule.
- Summarize project progress, financials, or team performance automatically.
- Reduce manual effort and improve accuracy in decision-making.

In this chapter, we will explore how to configure scheduled summaries in Smartsheet, automate report distribution, and ensure seamless data tracking.

1. Understanding Scheduled Summaries in Smartsheet

Smartsheet's **Scheduled Summaries** allow users to automate the generation and delivery of reports at predefined intervals. These reports can be customized to track key metrics, such as:

- **Project completion rates**
- **Budget utilization**
- **Task progress and overdue assignments**
- **Customer service response times**

Scheduled Summaries ensure that **decision-makers have real-time data** without having to manually compile reports.

2. Creating an Automated Report in Smartsheet

To streamline reporting, follow these steps to create and automate a scheduled summary:

Step 1: Create a Report in Smartsheet

1. **Click on the Smartsheet Home Page.**
2. Select **Create → Report → Row Report**.
3. Choose the source **Sheets** that contain the data you want to track.
4. **Apply Filters** to display relevant data (e.g., show only tasks due in the next week).
5. **Customize Columns** to include necessary fields such as Task Name, Assigned To, Due Date, and Status.
6. Click **Save** and name the report (e.g., "Weekly Project Summary").

3. Scheduling Automatic Report Delivery

Once the report is created, schedule it to be sent automatically to stakeholders.

Steps to Automate Report Delivery

1. Open the report and click **File → Send as Attachment**.
2. In the **Delivery Settings**, choose **Schedule Delivery**.

3. Set the **Delivery Frequency** (e.g., Daily, Weekly, Monthly).
4. Select the **Format** (PDF, Excel, or CSV).
5. Enter **Recipient Emails** (team members, executives, or clients).
6. Click **Save** to activate the scheduled report.

Example: Automating a Weekly Project Progress Report

- **Trigger:** Every Monday at 8 AM.
- **Report Format:** PDF summary of open and completed tasks.
- **Recipients:** Project Manager, Team Leads, Senior Executives.

This ensures that key stakeholders receive up-to-date project insights without manual effort.

---

4. Using Dashboard Widgets for Automated Summaries

Instead of relying solely on emailed reports, Smartsheet allows you to display scheduled summaries **directly on dashboards** using widgets.

Steps to Add a Summary Widget to a Dashboard

1. Open a Smartsheet **Dashboard**.
2. Click **Add Widget** → **Report Widget**.
3. Select the **Scheduled Report** from your saved reports.
4. Customize the widget layout and size.
5. Click **Save** to display the summary on the dashboard.

Example: Tracking Team Performance via Dashboard

- **Report Widget:** Displays weekly team task completion rates.
- **Graph Widget:** Shows pending vs. completed tasks in a visual format.
- **Live Data Refresh:** Automatically updates based on the latest report.

By embedding reports in dashboards, executives and managers can access **real-time insights** without waiting for scheduled emails.

---

5. Customizing Scheduled Summaries for Different Use Cases

Smartsheet allows you to **tailor automated reports** to meet various business needs.

a) Project Management Reporting

- Automatically send a summary of overdue tasks every Friday.
- Track project milestones and deliverables weekly.

b) Financial Reporting

- Generate and send a monthly **Budget vs. Actuals** report to the finance team.
- Automate invoice tracking and outstanding payment reminders.

c) HR and Employee Tracking

- Send a weekly **Employee Performance Summary** to HR managers.
- Automate onboarding progress tracking for new hires.

d) Customer Support & Service Metrics

- Generate a daily **Customer Support Ticket Report** for service managers.
- Track response time and resolution rates automatically.

These scheduled reports **enhance transparency, accountability, and efficiency across departments**.

---

6. Managing and Modifying Scheduled Reports

After setting up automated reporting, you may need to make adjustments over time.

a) Editing an Existing Scheduled Report

1. Open the **Reports** section in Smartsheet.
2. Select the report you want to modify.
3. Click **Edit Report Settings** to update filters, columns, or delivery schedules.
4. Save the changes to apply them immediately.

b) Disabling or Deleting a Scheduled Report

- Toggle **Scheduled Delivery** OFF to pause report distribution.
- Click **Delete Schedule** if the report is no longer needed.

Automation Tip: **Regularly review scheduled reports to ensure they remain relevant and align with business goals.**

---

7. Best Practices for Automating Reports and Summaries

To maximize the impact of automated reports, follow these best practices:

- **Keep reports concise** – Focus on key insights to avoid overwhelming recipients.
- **Use filters wisely** – Ensure reports only display relevant data.
- **Choose the right delivery format** – Use PDFs for executive summaries and Excel for detailed analysis.
- **Schedule reports at optimal times** – Deliver reports when stakeholders are most likely to review them.
- **Integrate with dashboards** – Combine scheduled summaries with live widgets for real-time tracking.

Conclusion

Automating reporting with **Scheduled Summaries** in Smartsheet ensures that businesses receive timely insights without the burden of manual compilation. By leveraging scheduled delivery, dashboard widgets, and customized reports, teams can make **data-driven decisions efficiently**.

Section 4:
Advanced Automation Techniques

Combining Multiple Automation Tools for Complex Workflows

As organizations scale, managing workflows becomes more complex, requiring multiple automation tools to work together seamlessly. While Smartsheet offers powerful standalone automation capabilities, combining multiple automation tools enables businesses to create **end-to-end** workflows that reduce manual work, enhance efficiency, and ensure smoother operations.

This chapter will guide you through **integrating multiple Smartsheet automation features**—such as workflow triggers, formulas, conditional logic, and third-party integrations—to build **advanced, interconnected workflows** tailored to your needs.

1. Why Combine Multiple Automation Tools?

Using a single automation feature in Smartsheet—such as an alert or approval workflow—is effective for simple tasks. However, **complex business processes** require multiple automation tools working in sync.

Benefits of combining automation tools:

- **Eliminate bottlenecks:** Automate sequential processes that involve multiple teams.
- **Improve data accuracy:** Reduce manual entry by connecting forms, sheets, and reports.
- **Ensure accountability:** Trigger approvals and notifications dynamically.
- **Enhance scalability:** Manage large-scale operations without increasing workload.

Example:

- A **form submission** triggers **task assignment**, which updates **status fields**, sends **notifications**, and generates **automated reports**—all without manual intervention.

2. Building a Multi-Layered Automation Workflow in Smartsheet

Let's explore how to **combine different automation tools** to streamline a multi-step workflow.

Step 1: Automate Data Entry with Forms

1. **Create a Smartsheet Form** for data collection (e.g., IT support requests, project proposals).
2. Ensure key fields such as **Requester Name, Priority, and Department** are included.
3. Enable **automatic row addition** when a form is submitted.

Step 2: Assign Tasks Based on Conditions

1. Click **Automation → Create Workflow**.
2. Set the trigger as **"When a row is added"** (new form submission).
3. Define conditions:

      ○ If **Priority = High**, assign to Senior Manager.
      ○ If **Priority = Low**, assign to Junior Analyst.
4. Update the **Assigned To** column dynamically.

Step 3: Automate Notifications to Keep Teams Informed

1. Click **Automation → Create Workflow → Send an Alert**.
2. Trigger: **When "Assigned To" is updated.**
3. Send a customized email notification to the assigned team member.
4. Include task details such as **due date, request type, and comments**.

Step 4: Use Conditional Logic to Manage Status Updates

1. Create an **Approval Workflow** to route approvals automatically.
2. If the **Status** column changes to **"Completed"**, trigger a notification to the requester.
3. If the **Status** is **"Pending Review"** for more than 3 days, escalate the task to a supervisor.

Step 5: Generate Automated Reports for Insights

1. Create a **Report** filtering only **Pending or Overdue tasks**.
2. Schedule **Weekly Summaries** to be sent automatically to managers.
3. Embed the report in a **Smartsheet Dashboard** for real-time tracking.

---

3. Advanced Use Cases for Combining Automation Tools

Smartsheet's automation features can be extended for **cross-functional workflows** involving multiple teams.

a) IT Support Ticketing System

Tools Used:

- **Forms** → Capture user-reported issues.
- **Automated Assignments** → Assign tickets based on category.
- **Status Updates & Reminders** → Notify IT support when deadlines approach.
- **Report Generation** → Summarize resolved and pending issues.

b) Employee Onboarding Workflow

Tools Used:

- **Forms** → New hire information collection.
- **Task Assignments** → Assign setup tasks to HR, IT, and managers.
- **Conditional Logic** → Send reminders for pending approvals.
- **Scheduled Reports** → Track onboarding progress.

c) Financial Invoice Approval Process

Tools Used:

- **Form Submissions** → Vendors submit invoice requests.
- **Conditional Approvals** → Invoices over $5,000 require executive approval.
- **Notifications** → Notify finance team on approval.
- **Automated Reporting** → Generate monthly invoice summary.

---

4. Integrating Smartsheet Automation with External Tools

While Smartsheet offers powerful built-in automation, integrating **third-party tools** expands capabilities even further.

a) Using Zapier to Connect Smartsheet with Other Apps

Zapier enables **Smartsheet integrations** with tools such as:

- **Google Sheets** (Sync real-time data updates)
- **Slack** (Send automated task notifications)
- **Trello or Jira** (Sync project tasks)
- **Salesforce** (Manage CRM updates)

Example:

- When a **new Smartsheet row is added**, Zapier triggers a **Slack message** and updates a **Google Sheet summary**.

b) Integrating with Microsoft Teams

- Post real-time Smartsheet updates in a **Teams Channel**.
- Notify teams when a **project milestone is completed**.

c) Leveraging the Smartsheet API for Custom Workflows

For businesses requiring **full customization**, the **Smartsheet API** allows:

- Automating data transfers between Smartsheet and databases.
- Creating complex approval flows integrating multiple departments.
- Customizing reports beyond Smartsheet's default capabilities.

---

5. Managing and Optimizing Complex Automation Workflows

As automation workflows grow, **managing complexity** becomes crucial.

a) Best Practices for Managing Multi-Step Automations

- **Label workflows clearly** to avoid confusion (e.g., "HR-Onboarding-Step1").
- **Test workflows in a sandbox environment** before deploying live.
- **Limit notification overload** by setting up only necessary alerts.
- **Use dependencies wisely** to prevent conflicts in automation logic.

b) Troubleshooting Common Issues in Multi-Step Workflows

- **Issue:** Task assignment fails.
  - **Solution:** Ensure the "Assigned To" column is formatted correctly.
- **Issue:** Notifications are sent multiple times.
  - **Solution:** Adjust trigger conditions to prevent redundant alerts.
- **Issue:** Approvals are delayed.
  - **Solution:** Set up **reminder escalations** for pending approvals.

Conclusion

Combining multiple automation tools in Smartsheet allows teams to build **powerful, end-to-end workflows** that eliminate manual processes and enhance efficiency. Whether integrating forms, task assignments, approvals, notifications, reports, or external tools like Zapier, Smartsheet provides a **scalable solution for automation-driven businesses**.

Leveraging Formulas for Dynamic Automation

While Smartsheet offers powerful built-in automation workflows, leveraging **formulas** can take automation to the next level by enabling **dynamic calculations, conditional updates, and real-time data manipulation**. By integrating formulas with automation workflows, teams can **automate decision-making processes, enhance reporting, and create smarter workflows**.

This chapter will guide you through:

- Understanding how formulas enhance Smartsheet automation.
- Commonly used formulas for automation.
- Using formulas for conditional triggers, automated calculations, and reporting.
- Best practices for combining formulas with automation workflows.

1. Why Use Formulas for Automation?

Formulas in Smartsheet are essential for **real-time data updates, logic-based automation, and reducing manual work**. They can be used to:

■ **Automate Status Updates:** Change task status based on due dates.
■ **Track Deadlines Dynamically:** Identify overdue tasks automatically.
■ **Calculate Progress Automatically:** Update project completion percentages.
■ **Trigger Alerts Based on Data Changes:** Notify users when conditions are met.
■ **Create Logical Conditions:** Automate approval processes based on form responses.

By combining Smartsheet formulas with automation workflows, teams can **automate more complex, data-driven decisions**.

2. Commonly Used Smartsheet Formulas for Automation

a) IF Statements for Conditional Automation

```
=IF([Status]@row = "Completed", "Archived", "Active")
```
■ Automatically categorizes tasks as **Archived** if marked **Completed**.

b) TODAY() for Date-Based Automation

```
=IF([Due Date]@row < TODAY(), "Overdue", "On Track")
```
■ Dynamically updates task status to **Overdue** when the due date passes.

c) COUNTIF for Tracking Pending Items

```
=COUNTIF([Status]:[Status], "Pending")
```
■ Counts all **Pending** tasks in a sheet for real-time reporting.

d) NETWORKDAYS for Business Days Calculation

```
=NETWORKDAYS([Start Date]@row, [End Date]@row)
```
■ Calculates **working days** between two dates, excluding weekends.

e) INDEX & MATCH for Dynamic Lookups
```
=INDEX([Assigned To]:[Assigned To], MATCH("IT Support", [Department]:[Department], 0))
```

■ Automatically assigns tasks to **specific team members** based on department.

By embedding these formulas within your sheets, Smartsheet can dynamically update values, which can **trigger automation workflows**.

---

3. Using Formulas to Trigger Automation Workflows

Smartsheet allows automation workflows to be **triggered based on formula-driven changes**.

Example: Automating Status Changes Based on Due Dates

1. Use the formula:
   `=IF([Due Date]@row < TODAY(), "Overdue", "On Track")`
2. Set up an automation workflow:
   - Trigger: **When the "Status" column changes.**
   - Condition: If **Status = "Overdue".**
   - Action: **Send an alert to the assigned user.**

🚀 **Result:** Whenever a task becomes overdue, an automatic **reminder is sent to the assigned user.**

---

4. Automating Progress Tracking with Formulas

Formulas can dynamically update **progress tracking** for projects.

Example: Auto-Calculating Project Completion %

Formula:

=COUNTIF([Task Status]:[Task Status], "Completed") / COUNT([Task Status]:[Task Status]) * 100

- This formula calculates the **percentage of tasks completed** in a project.
- The result can be displayed on **Smartsheet Dashboards** for real-time tracking.

Automation Workflow:

- **Trigger:** When "Completion %" column reaches **100%**.
- **Action:** Send a **notification** to project managers confirming project completion.

🚀 **Result: Automated progress tracking** ensures stakeholders stay informed **without manual updates**.

---

5. Using Formulas to Automate Task Prioritization

Formulas can categorize and prioritize tasks automatically based on deadlines and urgency.

Example: Auto-Prioritizing Tasks Based on Due Dates

Formula:

=IF([Due Date]@row < TODAY(), "Urgent", IF([Due Date]@row <= TODAY() + 3, "High", "Normal"))

- Tasks **past due** are marked as **Urgent**.
- Tasks **due within 3 days** are marked as **High** priority.
- All other tasks remain **Normal**.

Automation Workflow:

- **Trigger:** When **Priority** changes to "Urgent."
- **Action:** Send an **alert to the manager** and assign to a senior team member.

🚀 **Result: Proactive task management**, ensuring urgent issues are addressed immediately.

---

6. Automating Data Summaries for Reports

Smartsheet formulas can **auto-generate reports** without manual data entry.

Example: Counting Open Issues Per Department

Formula:

=COUNTIFS([Department]:[Department], "Finance", [Status]:[Status], "Open")

- Counts **open issues** in the **Finance** department.
- Can be used in **automated weekly reports**.

Automation Workflow:

- **Trigger:** Every **Monday at 9 AM**.
- **Action:** Send a **report** to department heads with open issues count.

🚀 **Result: Real-time issue tracking**, reducing dependency on manual reporting.

---

7. Best Practices for Using Formulas in Automation

1. **Keep formulas simple & scalable** – Complex formulas can slow down large sheets.
2. **Use helper columns** – Break down complex formulas into smaller calculations.
3. **Regularly test automation workflows** – Ensure formula-driven changes trigger expected actions.
4. **Combine formulas with Smartsheet dashboards** – Provide real-time project insights.
5. **Use cross-sheet formulas** – Link data across multiple Smartsheets for consolidated reporting.

Conclusion

Leveraging Smartsheet formulas for **dynamic automation** enhances efficiency, **reduces manual updates**, and improves decision-making. By **combining formulas with automation workflows**, teams can **automate status updates, progress tracking, prioritization, and reporting** effortlessly.

Implementing Conditional Logic in Automations

Automation in Smartsheet becomes significantly more powerful when **conditional logic** is applied. Instead of creating rigid, one-size-fits-all workflows, conditional logic allows automation to adapt based on specific conditions, ensuring **smarter, more efficient decision-making**.

With conditional logic, you can:
- **Route approvals based on form responses.**
- **Trigger different actions based on priority levels.**
- **Automatically categorize tasks based on due dates.**
- **Send alerts to different users depending on conditions.**

This chapter will explore how to **implement conditional logic** in Smartsheet automations, along with best practices for using it effectively.

---

1. Understanding Conditional Logic in Smartsheet Automations

Conditional logic allows **"If-Then" rules** to determine what happens when a trigger occurs. Instead of applying the same automation to every row, Smartsheet evaluates **specific conditions** before taking action.

For example:

- If a **task is overdue**, notify the project manager.
- If an **expense is over $5,000**, send it for executive approval.
- If a **support ticket is marked as urgent**, escalate it immediately.

These dynamic workflows **reduce manual intervention** and ensure **only relevant automations** are triggered.

---

2. Adding Conditional Logic to Smartsheet Automations

Smartsheet allows **conditions** to be added within an automation workflow. Here's how to apply them:

Step 1: Create a New Automation

1. Open your Smartsheet and go to **Automation**.
2. Click **Create Workflow** → Choose a trigger (e.g., **When a row is added/changed**).

Step 2: Define Conditions

1. Click **Add Condition**.
2. Choose a column and set a condition (e.g., "If Priority = High").
3. Add multiple conditions if needed (e.g., "AND Status = Pending").

Step 3: Define Actions Based on Conditions

1. If conditions are **met**, choose an action (e.g., **Send Notification** or **Move Row**).
2. If conditions are **not met**, set an alternative action or do nothing.
3. Click **Save** and activate the workflow.

- **Result:** The workflow will run **only when the defined conditions are true**.

3. Use Cases for Conditional Logic in Automation

Conditional logic makes Smartsheet automation more **intelligent** and **responsive**. Below are some common use cases.

a) Automating Task Prioritization

- **Trigger:** When a new task is created.
- **Condition:** If "Due Date" is within 3 days.
- **Action:** Set "Priority" column to **High** and notify the manager.

■ **Benefit:** Automatically prioritizes tasks based on deadlines.

b) Dynamic Approval Routing Based on Amount

- **Trigger:** When an expense request is submitted.
- **Condition 1:** If Amount ≤ **$1,000**, auto-approve.
- **Condition 2:** If Amount > **$1,000**, send to Finance Manager.
- **Condition 3:** If Amount > **$5,000**, require Executive approval.

■ **Benefit:** Ensures appropriate approvals without manual sorting.

c) Escalating Overdue Tasks

- **Trigger:** When a task remains incomplete for 3+ days.
- **Condition:** If "Status" is NOT "Completed."
- **Action:** Notify the project lead and **reassign task** to a senior team member.

■ **Benefit:** Reduces missed deadlines and improves accountability.

d) Auto-Categorizing Customer Support Tickets

- **Trigger:** When a new support ticket is logged.
- **Condition 1:** If "Urgency" = "High," assign to **Tier 2 Support**.
- **Condition 2:** If "Urgency" = "Low," assign to **Tier 1 Support**.
- **Condition 3:** If no response in 48 hours, escalate to manager.

■ **Benefit:** Streamlines support processes and reduces response time.

4. Combining Conditional Logic with Other Automation Features

Conditional logic works even better when combined with **other automation tools**.

a) Combining with Scheduled Automations

- **Example: Every Friday**, send a report listing all "High-Priority" tasks that are still open.

b) Combining with Alerts & Reminders

- Example: If a task is **still pending** 2 days before its due date, send a reminder.

c) Combining with Form Submissions

- Example: If a **form response** selects "Urgent," assign the request immediately.

---

5. Best Practices for Using Conditional Logic in Smartsheet Automations

1. **Use Simple Conditions First** – Start with basic "If-Then" conditions before adding complexity.
2. **Avoid Overloading Conditions** – Too many conditions can make automation difficult to manage.
3. **Test Before Deploying** – Run test cases to ensure the automation logic works as expected.
4. **Combine with Reports & Dashboards** – Track automation results using Smartsheet dashboards.
5. **Regularly Review & Optimize** – Adjust automation workflows as business needs change.

Conclusion

Conditional logic enhances Smartsheet automation by **enabling smart decision-making** based on data. By setting up **rule-based workflows**, businesses can **prioritize tasks, route approvals dynamically, escalate urgent issues, and automate repetitive actions** more effectively.

Integrating Smartsheet with Zapier

Smartsheet is a powerful platform for managing work and automating workflows, but its capabilities can be **greatly expanded** by integrating it with third-party apps. **Zapier**, a no-code automation tool, allows you to connect Smartsheet with **thousands of other applications**, such as Google Sheets, Slack, Trello, Jira, and Salesforce.

By integrating Smartsheet with Zapier, you can:
- **Sync data automatically between different platforms**
- **Trigger actions in other apps based on Smartsheet updates**
- **Eliminate repetitive manual tasks across multiple tools**
- **Streamline communication and project tracking**

This chapter will guide you through **how to connect Smartsheet with Zapier, common automation use cases, and best practices** to maximize efficiency.

---

1. What is Zapier and How Does It Work?

Zapier is a **workflow automation tool** that connects different apps through "Zaps"—automated workflows triggered by events in one app that perform actions in another.

Key Terms in Zapier Integration:

- **Trigger:** An event in Smartsheet that starts an automation (e.g., a new row is added).
- **Action:** The resulting task performed in another app (e.g., creating a Trello card).
- **Zap:** The automated workflow combining a trigger and an action.

Example:

- **Trigger:** A new task is assigned in Smartsheet.
- **Action:** A Slack message is sent to the assigned user.

🚀 **Result:** The team is instantly notified when tasks are assigned.

---

2. How to Connect Smartsheet to Zapier

Step 1: Sign Up for Zapier

1. Go to [Zapier's website] (https://zapier.com) and create an account.
2. Click **Make a Zap** to create a new automation.

Step 2: Choose Smartsheet as the Trigger App

1. In Zapier, search for **Smartsheet** and select it.
2. Choose a **Trigger Event** (e.g., "New Row" or "Updated Row").
3. Connect your **Smartsheet account** by logging in.

Step 3: Select a Trigger Sheet

1. Choose the Smartsheet file where the automation should apply.
2. Specify trigger conditions (e.g., "Trigger when a new task is added").

Step 4: Select the Action App

1. Search for the app where you want data to be sent (e.g., Slack, Trello, Google Sheets).
2. Choose the **Action Event** (e.g., "Send Message" or "Create Task").

Step 5: Customize the Action

1. Map fields from Smartsheet to the action app (e.g., Task Name → Trello Card Title).
2. Test the automation to ensure it works correctly.

Step 6: Activate the Zap

1. Click **Turn on Zap** to start the automation.
2. Monitor Zapier to ensure the workflow runs smoothly.

■ **Result:** Your Smartsheet data now automatically interacts with other apps without manual intervention.

---

3. Common Smartsheet + Zapier Use Cases

Smartsheet integrations can automate workflows across various business functions.

a) Project Management Integrations

■ **Trello/Jira:** Create a new Trello or Jira task when a new row is added in Smartsheet.
■ **Asana:** Sync Smartsheet task updates with Asana for better task tracking.

Example Zap:

- **Trigger:** A new task is added in Smartsheet.
- **Action:** A Trello card is created with the same details.

🚀 **Result:** Teams using Trello get instant updates without manual entry.

---

b) Team Communication Automations

■ **Slack:** Send a message in Slack when a task is assigned in Smartsheet.
■ **Microsoft Teams:** Notify a channel when a Smartsheet row is updated.

Example Zap:

- **Trigger:** A row in Smartsheet is marked "Completed."
- **Action:** A Slack message is sent to the project team.

🚀 **Result:** Team members are notified instantly about project progress.

---

c) Sales & CRM Syncing

■ **Salesforce/HubSpot:** Update CRM records when new client details are added in Smartsheet.
■ **Google Sheets:** Automatically sync Smartsheet data with Google Sheets for reporting.

Example Zap:

- **Trigger:** A new client entry is added to Smartsheet.
- **Action:** Salesforce updates the CRM with the client details.

✈ **Result:** No need for manual data entry between Smartsheet and Salesforce.

---

d) Reporting & Documentation

■ **Google Drive/Dropbox:** Save Smartsheet rows as PDFs in Google Drive.
■ **Google Sheets:** Append new Smartsheet data to an existing Google Sheet for reporting.

Example Zap:

- **Trigger:** A new Smartsheet report is generated.
- **Action:** The report is saved in Google Drive as a PDF.

✈ **Result:** Automated documentation reduces file management workload.

---

4. Advanced Smartsheet + Zapier Workflows

For more complex workflows, Zapier allows **multi-step automations**.

a) Multi-Step Approval Workflows

1. **Trigger:** A new expense request is submitted in Smartsheet.
2. **Action 1:** A Slack message is sent to the finance team.
3. **Action 2:** A task is created in Asana for approval.
4. **Action 3:** If approved, the request is logged in QuickBooks.

✈ **Result: End-to-end approval workflows without manual follow-ups.**

---

b) Conditional Automations with Filters

Zapier allows conditions to **filter data** before executing actions.

Example:

- **Trigger:** A new Smartsheet row is added.
- **Condition:** If the **budget is greater than $10,000**, send to the VP for approval.
- **Action:** If true, send an email; if false, send to the finance team.

✈ **Result:** Only relevant approvals are escalated to the VP.

---

5. Managing and Optimizing Zapier Integrations

Once Zapier automations are running, they require **regular maintenance**.

a) Monitoring & Troubleshooting

- Check the **Zapier Task History** for errors.
- Enable **Zapier Alerts** to notify you when a Zap fails.

b) Optimizing Performance

- Consolidate multiple Zaps into **one multi-step Zap** to reduce processing time.

- Use **Zapier Paths** for different automation conditions.
- Set **Zap Triggers to run on changes**, not every update, to save resources.

c) Keeping Integrations Secure

- Use **Zapier Admin Controls** to manage team access.
- Ensure **API permissions** are correctly set in Smartsheet and other apps.

🚀 **Result:** Your Smartsheet workflows remain reliable and scalable.

---

6. Best Practices for Smartsheet + Zapier Integration

▪ **Start with simple Zaps** before building complex multi-step workflows.
▪ **Test Zaps before activating** them in a live environment.
▪ **Use filters** to process only relevant Smartsheet rows.
▪ **Limit unnecessary notifications** to avoid spam alerts.
▪ **Review Zaps regularly** to ensure they remain relevant.

Conclusion

Integrating Smartsheet with Zapier **expands automation possibilities**, allowing seamless connections with **project management, sales, reporting, and communication tools**. By setting up **intelligent, automated workflows**, businesses can **save time, reduce errors, and improve efficiency**.

Connecting Smartsheet to Microsoft Teams

Microsoft Teams is one of the most widely used collaboration tools for organizations. By integrating Smartsheet with Microsoft Teams, teams can **enhance communication, streamline project tracking, and automate updates** without switching between applications.

This integration allows users to:
- ■ Receive **real-time notifications** in Teams when changes occur in Smartsheet.
- ■ Collaborate on Smartsheet projects directly within **Teams channels**.
- ■ Share **Smartsheet reports, sheets, and dashboards** in Teams.
- ■ Automate updates and alerts based on **Smartsheet workflows**.

In this chapter, we will cover **how to connect Smartsheet to Microsoft Teams, key use cases, and best practices** for leveraging this integration effectively.

---

1. Benefits of Integrating Smartsheet with Microsoft Teams

By linking Smartsheet with Microsoft Teams, organizations can **reduce communication delays and ensure stakeholders stay informed in real-time**.

Key benefits include:

- 📌 **Instant notifications** when changes happen in Smartsheet.
- ■ **Seamless collaboration** by accessing Smartsheet directly in Teams.
- ■ **Better visibility** with reports and dashboards embedded in Teams.
- ⚡ **Increased efficiency** by reducing the need to check Smartsheet manually.

---

2. How to Connect Smartsheet to Microsoft Teams

To set up the integration, follow these steps:

Step 1: Install the Smartsheet App in Microsoft Teams

1. Open **Microsoft Teams**.
2. Click on **Apps** (bottom-left corner).
3. Search for **Smartsheet** in the App Store.
4. Click **Add to a Team** and choose the relevant Teams **channel**.
5. Grant Smartsheet the necessary permissions when prompted.

Step 2: Sign in to Smartsheet from Teams

1. Open the Smartsheet app within Teams.
2. Click **Sign in with Smartsheet** and enter your credentials.
3. Allow Microsoft Teams to access Smartsheet data.

■ **Result:** Smartsheet is now integrated into your Microsoft Teams environment.

---

3. Setting Up Smartsheet Notifications in Teams

Smartsheet allows users to **send automatic updates to Teams channels** when specific actions occur.

Steps to Create an Automated Notification in Teams

1. **Open your Smartsheet** and click on **Automation**.
2. Click **Create Workflow** → **Send Alert**.
3. **Set the trigger** (e.g., "When a row is changed" or "When a new task is assigned").
4. **Select "Post a Message to Teams"** as the action.
5. Choose the **Teams channel** where the message should be sent.
6. Customize the **message format** to include relevant details (e.g., task name, due date).
7. Click **Save & Activate**.

🚀 **Example Use Case:**

- **Trigger:** When a project milestone is completed in Smartsheet.
- **Action:** A message is posted in the "Project Updates" Teams channel.
- **Result:** The entire team is instantly notified of milestone progress.

---

4. Embedding Smartsheet Dashboards in Teams

For **real-time visibility**, you can embed **Smartsheet dashboards and reports** directly into Microsoft Teams.

Steps to Add a Smartsheet Dashboard to Teams

1. Open **Microsoft Teams** and go to the desired **channel**.
2. Click the **+ (Add a tab)** button.
3. Select **Smartsheet** from the list of apps.
4. Choose **Dashboard, Report, or Sheet**.
5. Select the Smartsheet item you want to embed.
6. Click **Save**.

⬛ **Result:** Team members can now view Smartsheet data **without leaving Teams**.

🚀 **Example Use Case:**

- The **marketing team** adds a Smartsheet dashboard in Teams to **track campaign performance in real time**.

---

5. Using Smartsheet Bots in Teams for Automated Interactions

Smartsheet's integration includes **bot functionality**, allowing users to receive updates and interact with Smartsheet directly within Teams.

How to Enable Smartsheet Bot Notifications

1. Open **Microsoft Teams**.
2. Go to **Apps** → Search for **Smartsheet Bot**.
3. Click **Add to Chat** and choose your Team.
4. Type **"help"** in the chat to see available commands.

⬛ **Result:** Team members can receive **personalized updates** or request Smartsheet data via chat.

🚀 **Example Use Case:**

- A team member types **"show my tasks"**, and the bot retrieves all tasks assigned to them in Smartsheet.

---

6. Advanced Automation: Combining Smartsheet, Microsoft Teams, and Power Automate

For **more complex workflows**, Smartsheet can be integrated with **Microsoft Power Automate** (previously Microsoft Flow) to:

- Sync data between Smartsheet and **Microsoft Planner**.
- Send Smartsheet updates via **Teams chat messages**.
- Automate task creation in Smartsheet based on **Teams activity**.

Example: Automating Smartsheet Task Creation from Teams Messages

- **Trigger:** A user posts a message in a Teams channel with a task request.
- **Action 1:** Power Automate extracts the task details.
- **Action 2:** A new task is created in Smartsheet with the extracted details.
- **Action 3:** A confirmation message is posted in Teams.

🚀 **Result:** Task requests made in Teams **automatically appear in Smartsheet**, reducing manual entry.

---

7. Best Practices for Using Smartsheet with Microsoft Teams

■ **Use notifications selectively** – Avoid excessive alerts to prevent notification fatigue.
■ **Assign specific channels for Smartsheet updates** – Keep project discussions organized.
■ **Train team members on Smartsheet-Teams workflows** – Ensure adoption of automation best practices.
■ **Regularly update dashboards and reports** – Keep Teams integrations relevant and useful.
■ **Combine with Power Automate for advanced workflows** – Unlock full automation potential.

Conclusion

Integrating **Smartsheet with Microsoft Teams** enhances **collaboration, communication, and project visibility**. By leveraging **automated notifications, embedded dashboards, and chatbot interactions**, teams can **work more efficiently without switching between tools**.

Leveraging Smartsheet with Slack

Slack is a widely used communication tool that helps teams collaborate efficiently. By integrating **Smartsheet with Slack**, teams can **automate task notifications, streamline approvals, and ensure real-time project updates** without switching between apps.

This integration allows you to:
- Receive **instant alerts** in Slack when updates occur in Smartsheet.
- Automatically **notify team members** of assigned tasks.
- Share **Smartsheet reports, sheets, and dashboards** within Slack.
- Set up **workflow automation** to keep Slack channels updated with project progress.

This chapter will cover **how to connect Smartsheet to Slack, key automation use cases, and best practices** for optimizing collaboration.

1. Why Integrate Smartsheet with Slack?

Connecting Smartsheet with Slack ensures that teams stay updated **without needing to check Smartsheet manually**.

Key benefits include:

- 🔔 **Real-time notifications** when tasks or projects are updated.
- 🚀 **Faster approvals** by sending approval requests directly to Slack.
- **Improved visibility** by sharing Smartsheet data in Slack channels.
- **Enhanced team collaboration** by reducing back-and-forth emails.

Example Use Case:

- A **project manager updates a task in Smartsheet**, triggering an **automatic Slack notification** to the assigned user.

2. How to Connect Smartsheet to Slack

To set up the Smartsheet-Slack integration, follow these steps:

Step 1: Install the Smartsheet App in Slack

1. Open **Slack** and go to **Apps**.
2. Search for **Smartsheet** in the Slack App Directory.
3. Click **Add to Slack** and authorize the connection.

Step 2: Sign in to Smartsheet from Slack

1. Open the Smartsheet app within Slack.
2. Click **Connect Smartsheet Account** and log in with your credentials.
3. Grant **Slack permissions** to access your Smartsheet data.

Result: Smartsheet and Slack are now linked, allowing **data synchronization and automated updates**.

3. Automating Notifications from Smartsheet to Slack

One of the most powerful features of this integration is **sending automated Smartsheet notifications to Slack** when specific actions occur.

Steps to Set Up Smartsheet Notifications in Slack

1. Open **Smartsheet** and go to the **Automation tab**.
2. Click **Create Workflow → Send an Alert**.
3. **Set the trigger** (e.g., "When a row is added" or "When a task is marked completed").
4. **Select "Post a Message to Slack"** as the action.
5. Choose the **Slack channel or user** to receive notifications.
6. Customize the **message format** (e.g., include task name, due date, and status).
7. Click **Save & Activate**.

🚀 **Example Use Case:**

- **Trigger:** When a task is assigned to a user in Smartsheet.
- **Action:** A **Slack message** is sent to the user with task details.
- **Result:** The team member is **instantly notified** about new assignments.

---

4. Using Slack to Approve Smartsheet Requests

Slack can be used for **real-time approvals** from Smartsheet.

Steps to Enable Approvals in Slack

1. In Smartsheet, create a **new approval workflow**.
2. Set **Slack** as the approval method.
3. Define the **trigger event** (e.g., when an expense request is submitted).
4. Choose the **Slack user(s)** who will approve or reject the request.
5. Customize the **Slack message** (e.g., "Approve or Reject this request").
6. Click **Save & Activate**.

🚀 **Example Use Case:**

- **Trigger:** A new budget request is submitted in Smartsheet.
- **Action:** The request appears in Slack with **Approve/Reject** buttons.
- **Result:** Managers can **approve the request instantly from Slack** without opening Smartsheet.

---

5. Sharing Smartsheet Data in Slack

Instead of manually copying Smartsheet links, you can **embed sheets, reports, and dashboards** in Slack.

Steps to Share Smartsheet Data in Slack

1. Open a Smartsheet report or dashboard.
2. Click **Share → Copy the Smartsheet link**.
3. Paste the link into a Slack channel.
4. The link will **automatically generate a preview** in Slack.

◼ **Result:** Team members can **view and open Smartsheet data directly from Slack**.

🚀 **Example Use Case:**

- A **marketing team shares a campaign performance report** in Slack so stakeholders can review updates quickly.

---

6. Advanced Automation: Combining Smartsheet, Slack, and Zapier

For **more complex workflows**, you can connect Smartsheet and Slack using **Zapier** to trigger **multi-step automations**.

Example: Automating Slack Messages Based on Smartsheet Changes

- **Trigger:** A new Smartsheet row is added.
- **Condition:** If "Priority" is **High**, notify Slack.
- **Action:** Send a Slack alert to the team with task details.

🚀 **Result: Urgent tasks automatically notify** the right Slack channel.

Example: Creating Smartsheet Tasks from Slack Messages

- **Trigger:** A user posts "/newtask" in a Slack channel.
- **Action:** Zapier extracts task details and adds them to Smartsheet.

🚀 **Result:** New tasks from Slack discussions are **automatically added** to Smartsheet.

---

7. Best Practices for Using Smartsheet with Slack

■ **Avoid notification overload** – Only set up critical alerts to prevent Slack spam.
■ **Use dedicated Slack channels** – Keep Smartsheet updates organized by project or team.
■ **Leverage approvals in Slack** – Speed up decision-making with instant approvals.
■ **Train your team** – Ensure all members know how to use Smartsheet-Slack integrations effectively.
■ **Regularly update integrations** – Optimize workflows as your team's needs evolve.

Conclusion

Integrating **Smartsheet with Slack enhances collaboration, speeds up approvals, and ensures real-time updates**. By **leveraging automation, notifications, and shared data**, teams can **reduce manual work and improve efficiency**.

Using Smartsheet API for Custom Automations

While Smartsheet's built-in automation features are powerful, there are cases where **custom automations** are needed to achieve more complex workflows. This is where the **Smartsheet API** comes in. The **Smartsheet API** allows developers and power users to integrate Smartsheet with other applications, retrieve and update data programmatically, and create highly customized automation workflows.

With the **Smartsheet API**, you can:
■ **Automate bulk data entry and updates.**
■ **Connect Smartsheet with external applications** beyond built-in integrations.
■ **Trigger automations based on advanced logic** beyond Smartsheet's native capabilities.
■ **Generate custom reports and dashboards** dynamically.

In this chapter, we will cover:

- How to **set up and authenticate** the Smartsheet API.
- Common use cases for **custom automations**.
- Code examples for **automating tasks using Python**.
- Best practices for **using the Smartsheet API efficiently**.

1. Understanding the Smartsheet API

The **Smartsheet API** is a **RESTful API** that allows users to interact with Smartsheet programmatically. You can **retrieve, update, delete, and manipulate Smartsheet data** using API requests.

Key Features of the Smartsheet API

- **Retrieve data from sheets** (GET requests).
- **Update cells, rows, and columns** programmatically (PUT/POST requests).
- **Create new sheets and copy data** dynamically.
- **Trigger actions based on external events** (e.g., CRM or ERP system updates).
- **Integrate Smartsheet with databases** (MySQL, PostgreSQL, etc.).

Who Should Use the Smartsheet API?

The API is useful for **developers, IT admins, and advanced users** looking to build **custom integrations and automations** beyond what's possible with Smartsheet's built-in tools.

2. Setting Up and Authenticating the Smartsheet API

Step 1: Get Your Smartsheet API Key

1. Log in to your **Smartsheet account**.
2. Click on your profile picture (top right) → Select **Apps & Integrations**.
3. Under **API Access**, click **Generate new access token**.
4. Copy the API key and store it securely (this key is required for API authentication).

Step 2: Install Python and the Smartsheet SDK

If you plan to use Python to interact with the Smartsheet API, install the Smartsheet Python SDK:

```
pip install smartsheet-python-sdk
```

Step 3: Authenticate API Requests

To interact with Smartsheet, use the API key in your requests.

Example: Connecting to Smartsheet API in Python

```
import smartsheet

# Initialize Smartsheet API client
smartsheet_client = smartsheet.Smartsheet('YOUR_API_KEY')

# Verify API connection
account = smartsheet_client.Users.get_current_user()
print(f"Connected to Smartsheet as: {account.email}")
```

■ **Result:** If authentication is successful, it prints the Smartsheet account email.

---

3. Common Use Cases for Custom Automations

By leveraging the Smartsheet API, you can build **advanced automations** that Smartsheet's standard automation tools cannot handle.

a) Bulk Data Entry and Updates

■ Automatically update thousands of Smartsheet rows from an external database.

b) External System Integration

■ Sync Smartsheet data with **Salesforce, QuickBooks, or Jira** in real-time.

c) Custom Alerts and Notifications

■ Send personalized notifications to **WhatsApp, Slack, or Email** when specific conditions are met.

d) Data Backup and Exporting

■ Export Smartsheet data to **Google Sheets, CSV, or an SQL database** for backup or analytics.

---

4. Example API Automations with Python

Here are some **practical examples** of how to use the **Smartsheet API** for automation.

Example 1: Retrieving Data from a Smartsheet Sheet

```
sheet_id = 1234567890  # Replace with your actual sheet ID

# Retrieve sheet details
sheet = smartsheet_client.Sheets.get_sheet(sheet_id)

# Print sheet name and row count
print(f"Sheet Name: {sheet.name}, Total Rows: {sheet.total_row_count}")
```

■ **Result:** Displays the sheet name and the number of rows in the sheet.

Example 2: Automatically Adding Rows to a Smartsheet Sheet

```
new_row = smartsheet.models.Row()
new_row.to_top = True  # Add row to the top of the sheet

# Define row data
new_row.cells.append({"column_id": 987654321, "value": "New Task"})
new_row.cells.append({"column_id": 876543210, "value": "In Progress"})

# Add row to Smartsheet
smartsheet_client.Sheets.add_rows(sheet_id, [new_row])

print("New row added successfully!")
```

■ **Result:** A new task row is **automatically added** to the Smartsheet.

Example 3: Sending Slack Alerts When a Row is Updated

To send alerts when a Smartsheet row is updated, you can use **Zapier, Power Automate, or a custom webhook**.

```
import requests

SLACK_WEBHOOK_URL = "https://hooks.slack.com/services/YOUR/SLACK/WEBHOOK"

# Message format
message = {"text": "A new task has been assigned in Smartsheet!"}

# Send message to Slack
requests.post(SLACK_WEBHOOK_URL, json=message)

print("Slack notification sent!")
```

■ **Result:** Slack users receive a real-time **task assignment notification**.

---

5. Advanced API Use Cases

For more **complex** workflows, you can combine the **Smartsheet API with AI, machine learning, and cloud services**.

a) AI-Driven Task Prioritization

■ Use **AI-based sentiment analysis** to classify incoming customer service tickets in Smartsheet.

b) Automating Financial Reports

■ Generate monthly **financial summaries** in Smartsheet based on **QuickBooks or ERP data**.

c) Creating a Custom Dashboard

■ Pull Smartsheet data into **Google Data Studio or Power BI** for **real-time analytics**.

---

6. Best Practices for Using the Smartsheet API

To ensure **smooth API operations**, follow these best practices:

- **Use API Rate Limits Wisely** – Avoid excessive API calls to prevent throttling.
- **Secure API Keys** – Never share API keys publicly; use environment variables.
- **Implement Error Handling** – Catch API errors and retry failed requests.
- **Optimize Data Fetching** – Use **pagination** when retrieving large datasets.
- **Regularly Monitor API Performance** – Set up logging and alerts for API failures.

Conclusion

The **Smartsheet API** unlocks a new level of automation, allowing businesses to **customize workflows, integrate with external systems, and streamline operations** beyond built-in Smartsheet features.

By **leveraging Python, webhooks, and third-party integrations**, you can create **highly efficient automation workflows** that improve productivity and decision-making.

Section 5:
Real-World Applications and Use Cases

Automating Project Management Processes

Effective project management requires **planning, tracking, and communication** to ensure projects stay on schedule and within budget. Manual processes—such as updating tasks, assigning responsibilities, and tracking progress—can slow teams down and lead to errors. **Smartsheet automation** helps project managers eliminate repetitive tasks, streamline communication, and ensure project goals are met efficiently.

By **automating project management processes** in Smartsheet, teams can:
■ **Automatically assign tasks** based on project phases.
■ **Send real-time alerts** for approaching deadlines.
■ **Track project progress dynamically** with dashboards.
■ **Generate automated reports** for stakeholders.
■ **Integrate Smartsheet with project management tools** like Jira, Asana, or Trello.

This chapter will cover how to **set up automated project tracking, task management, approvals, and reporting** in Smartsheet to improve efficiency and reduce manual work.

---

1. Key Project Management Challenges That Automation Solves

Project managers often face the following challenges:

* **Task Assignments Take Time** – Manually assigning tasks can be inefficient.
* **Missed Deadlines** – Without timely reminders, critical deadlines can be overlooked.
* **Inefficient Approvals** – Waiting for manual approvals can delay project progress.
* **Lack of Real-Time Visibility** – Stakeholders often need up-to-date reports without manual updates.
* **Data Duplication** – Manually copying data between tools wastes time and increases errors.

■ **Smartsheet automation solves these issues by ensuring processes run smoothly, consistently, and with minimal human intervention.**

---

2. Automating Task Assignments and Dependencies

In project management, **assigning tasks efficiently** is crucial for keeping work on track. Smartsheet automation allows you to automatically assign tasks **based on predefined rules**.

Steps to Automate Task Assignments

1. Open your Smartsheet project plan and click **Automation → Create Workflow**.
2. Choose the trigger **"When a new row is added"** (i.e., when a new task is created).
3. Click **Add Condition**, then select:
   ○ If **Task Type = "Design"**, assign it to the Design Team.
   ○ If **Task Type = "Development"**, assign it to the Engineering Team.
4. Set the **Action** to **"Assign User"** by updating the "Assigned To" column.

5. Click **Save & Activate**.

🚀 **Result:** Whenever a new task is added, it is automatically assigned to the correct team based on its type.

---

3. Automating Project Status Updates

Manually updating project status can be time-consuming. Smartsheet can **automatically update task status** based on progress.

Example: Auto-Update Status Based on Completion Percentage

1. Add a **"Progress %" column** to your Smartsheet.
2. Create an automation workflow:
   ○ If **Progress = 100%**, change the **Status** to "Completed".
   ○ If **Progress = 50%**, change **Status** to "In Progress".
   ○ If **Progress < 25%**, set **Status** to "Not Started".

🚀 **Result:** The project status updates automatically as work progresses.

---

4. Automating Task Deadline Reminders

Missed deadlines can derail projects. Smartsheet can **send automatic alerts** before tasks are due.

Steps to Set Up Deadline Reminders

1. Click **Automation → Create Workflow → Send Alert**.
2. **Trigger:** "When Due Date is 3 days away".
3. **Condition: If Status is NOT Completed**.
4. **Action:** Send an alert to the assigned team member and project manager.
5. Click **Save & Activate**.

🚀 **Result:** Users get automated reminders before deadlines, reducing missed tasks.

---

5. Automating Project Approvals

Many projects require **stakeholder approvals** (e.g., design sign-offs, budget approvals). Smartsheet can automate the approval process to avoid delays.

Example: Auto-Approval Workflow

1. **Trigger:** When a row is added with a status of **"Pending Approval"**.
2. **Condition:** If **Budget > $10,000**, send approval request to **Senior Manager**.
3. **Action:**
   ○ Send an **approval request** email with "Approve" or "Decline" buttons.
   ○ If **approved**, update status to **"Approved"**.
   ○ If **declined**, update status to **"Revised Required"** and notify the requester.

🚀 **Result:** The approval process is automated, reducing waiting times.

---

6. Automating Project Reports and Dashboards

Stakeholders need real-time project updates without manually compiling reports. Smartsheet can **automate reporting and dashboards**.

Steps to Create Automated Project Reports

1. Create a **new report** to track project status, budget, and task completion.
2. Use filters to show **only active projects**.
3. Click **File → Schedule Report Delivery**.
4. Set a schedule (e.g., **Every Monday at 9 AM**).
5. Choose **Recipients** (e.g., Project Manager, Executives).
6. Click **Save & Activate**.

🚀 **Result:** Stakeholders receive **weekly project reports automatically**.

---

7. Integrating Smartsheet with Other Project Management Tools

Smartsheet integrates with **Jira, Trello, Microsoft Project, and Asana** to keep data synchronized across tools.

Example: Syncing Smartsheet with Jira for IT Project Management

- **Trigger:** When a task is added in Smartsheet.
- **Action:** Create a matching **Jira issue** automatically.
- **Result:** Engineering teams using Jira can track tasks without duplicating data.

■ This eliminates the need for manual updates between different platforms.

---

8. Best Practices for Automating Project Management in Smartsheet

■ **Keep automation simple** – Start with small automations before adding complexity.
■ **Use dependencies wisely** – Automate task sequences using predecessor logic.
■ **Test workflows regularly** – Ensure automations trigger correctly.
■ **Train your team** – Make sure users understand how automated workflows function.
■ **Monitor performance** – Use dashboards to track automation effectiveness.

Conclusion

Automating project management processes in Smartsheet **reduces manual work, improves efficiency, and ensures projects stay on track**. By leveraging **task automation, status updates, deadline reminders, approval workflows, and reporting**, teams can focus on **strategic work instead of administrative tasks**.

Enhancing Marketing Campaigns with Automation

Marketing campaigns require **extensive planning, execution, tracking, and optimization**. Managing campaigns manually—assigning tasks, tracking deliverables, updating stakeholders, and analyzing performance—can be time-consuming and error-prone. **Smartsheet automation** streamlines these processes, allowing marketing teams to **increase efficiency, reduce errors, and execute campaigns more effectively**.

By leveraging **Smartsheet automation**, marketing teams can:
- **Automate campaign planning** by using templates and predefined workflows.
- **Streamline task assignments** for content creation, approvals, and publishing.
- **Monitor campaign performance in real-time** with automated reports.
- **Send alerts and notifications** when deadlines approach.
- **Integrate with marketing tools** like Google Analytics, HubSpot, and social media platforms.

This chapter will cover **how to set up automated workflows for marketing campaigns, manage approvals, track performance, and integrate Smartsheet with marketing tools**.

---

1. Challenges in Marketing Campaign Management

Marketing teams often face the following challenges:

- **Campaign planning is time-consuming** – Assigning tasks, tracking deliverables, and setting timelines manually can be inefficient.
- **Approval processes slow execution** – Waiting for content or budget approvals delays progress.
- **Lack of real-time visibility** – Teams struggle to get **up-to-date campaign performance reports**.
- **Inconsistent communication** – Team members and stakeholders miss critical updates.
- **Manual data entry** – Entering and updating campaign performance metrics takes time.

- **Smartsheet automation solves these issues by ensuring marketing campaigns run smoothly with minimal manual intervention.**

---

2. Automating Campaign Planning with Smartsheet Templates

Marketing teams **frequently repeat similar campaign structures**, such as product launches, email campaigns, and social media promotions. Instead of starting from scratch each time, Smartsheet allows you to **use campaign templates with built-in automation**.

Steps to Automate Campaign Planning

1. Open **Smartsheet** and create a **Campaign Planning Sheet**.
2. Set up standard **task categories**:
   - Content creation
   - Social media scheduling
   - Email marketing
   - Ad campaign tracking
3. **Apply automation rules**:
   - When a new campaign starts, **automatically assign team members**.
   - Set up **reminders** for key milestones.
   - Trigger **status updates** based on task progress.

🚀 **Result:** Each time a new campaign is launched, Smartsheet automatically assigns responsibilities and schedules key tasks.

---

3. Automating Content Creation and Approval Workflows

Marketing campaigns often involve **blog posts, ads, social media graphics, and videos**—all of which require approvals before publication. Smartsheet can **automate the approval process**, reducing bottlenecks.

Example: Automating Content Approval Workflows

1. **Trigger:** A new content piece is submitted.
2. **Condition:** If content type is "Blog Post", assign to **Content Manager** for review.
3. **Action:**
   - If **approved**, update status to "Ready to Publish".
   - If **rejected**, notify the creator and move to "Revisions Needed".

🚀 **Result:** Content approvals are **streamlined**, reducing delays in publishing.

---

4. Automating Social Media and Email Marketing Schedules

Marketing teams manage multiple **social media platforms and email campaigns**. Smartsheet can automate scheduling and tracking.

Example: Social Media Scheduling Workflow

1. **Trigger:** A new post is scheduled in Smartsheet.
2. **Action:**
   - If the **post is for Twitter**, schedule a **Zapier automation** to publish it automatically.
   - If the **post is for LinkedIn**, send a **Slack notification** to the social media manager for approval.

🚀 **Result:** Social media posts **publish on time without manual intervention**.

Example: Automating Email Marketing Campaigns

1. **Trigger:** A new email campaign is planned in Smartsheet.
2. **Action:**
   - If the **email is ready**, update the "Scheduled Date" column.
   - If an **email campaign is overdue**, send a **reminder to the email team**.

🚀 **Result:** Email campaigns are launched on time with **automated reminders**.

---

5. Automating Marketing Campaign Performance Tracking

Marketing teams rely on **campaign performance data** from multiple sources. Instead of manually entering data, Smartsheet can pull in performance metrics automatically.

Example: Tracking Ad Performance Automatically

1. **Trigger:** Smartsheet connects to **Google Ads or Facebook Ads** using Zapier.
2. **Action:**

- Pull in metrics like **CTR, impressions, and conversions** every day.
- Update the Smartsheet **Campaign Performance Dashboard**.

🚀 **Result:** Teams get real-time **advertising performance updates** without manual reporting.

Example: Weekly Marketing Reports

1. **Trigger:** Every **Monday at 9 AM**.
2. **Action:**
   - Compile **weekly engagement metrics** from email, social media, and web analytics.
   - Send an **automated campaign report** to stakeholders.

🚀 **Result:** Marketing teams receive **weekly reports without manual work**.

---

6. Integrating Smartsheet with Other Marketing Tools

Smartsheet integrates with **marketing automation tools** like:
- ◼ **HubSpot** – Sync lead data and campaign results.
- ◼ **Google Analytics** – Pull web performance metrics into Smartsheet.
- ◼ **Salesforce** – Connect marketing and sales data.
- ◼ **Trello/Asana** – Sync campaign tasks between tools.

Example: Syncing Smartsheet with HubSpot for Lead Tracking

- **Trigger:** A new marketing lead is captured in HubSpot.
- **Action:** The lead is **added to Smartsheet**, where the team tracks engagement.

◼ **This ensures marketing and sales teams stay aligned** without manual data entry.

---

7. Best Practices for Automating Marketing Campaigns in Smartsheet

- ◼ **Use automation for repetitive tasks** – Set up workflows to handle scheduling and approvals.
- ◼ **Leverage Smartsheet dashboards** – Create live dashboards for campaign tracking.
- ◼ **Connect with analytics tools** – Integrate Smartsheet with Google Analytics, HubSpot, or other reporting tools.
- ◼ **Limit unnecessary notifications** – Avoid overwhelming team members with alerts.
- ◼ **Review automation workflows regularly** – Optimize automations based on feedback.

Conclusion

Automating marketing campaigns in Smartsheet **saves time, improves coordination, and enhances performance tracking**. By setting up **automated workflows for content approvals, social media scheduling, and campaign reporting**, marketing teams can focus on **strategy and creativity rather than manual tasks**.

Streamlining HR Onboarding Workflows

The **HR onboarding process** is critical to ensuring new employees have a smooth transition into an organization. However, onboarding often involves **multiple steps, documents, and approvals**, which can create inefficiencies if managed manually.

Smartsheet automation can **eliminate delays, ensure consistency, and improve the overall onboarding experience** by:
- Automatically **assigning onboarding tasks** to HR teams and new hires.
- Sending **reminders and follow-ups** for pending paperwork or training.
- Tracking **progress in real-time** with automated reports and dashboards.
- Ensuring **compliance** by storing documents securely and triggering approvals.

This chapter will cover how to **set up Smartsheet automation for onboarding workflows**, manage **HR tasks**, and integrate **Smartsheet with HR tools** to **reduce manual work and increase efficiency**.

---

1. Challenges in HR Onboarding That Automation Solves

- **Paperwork delays** – Manually tracking forms and documents slows the onboarding process.
- **Missed deadlines** – Without automated reminders, HR teams and new hires can forget critical tasks.
- **Inefficient approvals** – Waiting for managers to approve forms manually can cause bottlenecks.
- **Lack of visibility** – HR teams struggle to track which employees have completed onboarding steps.
- **Compliance risks** – Manual record-keeping increases the risk of non-compliance with HR policies.

By automating HR onboarding, Smartsheet ensures a **structured, efficient, and compliant process for new hires.**

---

2. Setting Up an Automated HR Onboarding Workflow in Smartsheet

The **HR onboarding workflow** consists of several steps, including document submission, training, IT setup, and first-week check-ins. Smartsheet automation ensures each step is completed on time.

Steps to Create an Automated Onboarding Workflow

1. **Create a Smartsheet onboarding tracker**
   - Columns: **Employee Name, Start Date, Status, Assigned HR Rep, Task List, Due Date, Completion %**
2. **Set up an automation to assign onboarding tasks**
   - **Trigger:** When a new employee is added to the Smartsheet.
   - **Action:** Automatically assign HR tasks such as:
     - Sending a welcome email
     - Assigning paperwork submission
     - Scheduling IT setup and training sessions
3. **Automate status updates based on task completion**
   - **Trigger:** When all tasks are marked complete.
   - **Action:** Update employee status to **"Onboarded"** and send a confirmation email to HR.

Result: Every new hire follows the same structured onboarding process, reducing manual tracking.

---

3. Automating Document Submission & Compliance

HR onboarding involves **collecting and verifying** key documents such as:
- Offer letters
- Tax forms (W-4, I-9, etc.)
- Non-disclosure agreements (NDAs)
- Training acknowledgments

Example: Automating HR Document Submission & Reminders

1. **Trigger:** When an employee is added to Smartsheet.
2. **Action:** Send an email with a list of required documents and upload links.
3. **Trigger:** If documents are **not submitted within 3 days**, send a **follow-up reminder**.
4. **Action:** Once all documents are uploaded, update the **status to "Complete"** and notify HR.

🚀 **Result:** HR no longer has to chase employees manually for missing documents.

4. Automating IT and Facilities Requests

HR onboarding isn't just about paperwork—it also involves **setting up IT access, provisioning devices, and arranging office space**. Smartsheet automation can trigger **IT and facilities tasks** for each new hire.

Example: Automating IT Setup for New Employees

1. **Trigger:** When a new hire is added to the Smartsheet.
2. **Action:**
   - Create a task for **IT to set up email, software, and security access**.
   - Create a request for **Facilities to assign a desk or send work-from-home equipment**.
3. **Trigger:** If IT setup is not completed **before start date**, send an **escalation reminder**.

🚀 **Result:** IT and Facilities teams receive **automated task assignments**, preventing last-minute delays.

5. Automating Training and Orientation Schedules

New hires typically go through **orientation sessions, compliance training, and job-specific training**. Smartsheet can automatically **schedule and track training completion**.

Example: Automating Training Assignments

1. **Trigger:** Employee **start date** arrives.
2. **Action:** Assign the employee to required training courses and add deadlines.
3. **Trigger:** If training is **not completed within 7 days**, send a **reminder**.
4. **Action:** If training is completed, update the **training status to "Complete"**.

🚀 **Result:** HR no longer has to manually track training completion—it's fully automated.

6. Tracking Onboarding Progress with Automated Dashboards

HR teams need a **clear overview** of onboarding progress to ensure every new hire is on track. Smartsheet can automatically **generate live dashboards** that show:
- Number of employees in onboarding
- Percentage of employees who completed onboarding
- Pending tasks for each new hire

Steps to Set Up an Automated Onboarding Dashboard

1. Create a **Smartsheet dashboard** with widgets for:
   - A **real-time onboarding tracker** (showing pending vs. completed tasks).
   - A **list of employees who need follow-ups**.
   - A **graph showing onboarding completion rate**.
2. Automate **dashboard updates** using real-time data from the onboarding tracker.
3. Share the dashboard with **HR, IT, and managers**.

🚀 **Result:** HR teams always have an up-to-date view of onboarding progress **without manual updates**.

---

7. Integrating Smartsheet with HR Systems (Workday, BambooHR, etc.)

Smartsheet integrates with **HR software** like:

■ **Workday** – Sync employee records and training progress.
■ **BambooHR** – Automate onboarding tasks and document collection.
■ **Google Workspace** – Create automatic email and calendar invites for new hires.

Example: Syncing Smartsheet with Workday for Onboarding

1. **Trigger:** A new hire is added to Workday.
2. **Action:** The employee's details are **synced to Smartsheet**, triggering the onboarding workflow.

🚀 **Result:** HR doesn't need to **manually enter employee details** into Smartsheet.

---

8. Best Practices for Automating HR Onboarding with Smartsheet

■ **Standardize onboarding templates** – Use the same automated process for all hires.
■ **Automate reminders** – Reduce follow-ups by sending alerts for incomplete tasks.
■ **Track onboarding metrics** – Use Smartsheet dashboards to monitor onboarding efficiency.
■ **Integrate with HR software** – Reduce manual data entry by syncing Smartsheet with HR tools.
■ **Regularly update workflows** – Optimize automation rules based on HR feedback.

Conclusion

Automating HR onboarding with Smartsheet **eliminates inefficiencies, improves compliance, and enhances the employee experience.** By **automating tasks, tracking progress, and integrating with HR software**, organizations can streamline the onboarding process while ensuring new hires are set up for success.

Optimizing Operations in Manufacturing

Manufacturing operations involve **complex workflows, production tracking, inventory management, quality control, and compliance monitoring**. Managing these processes manually can lead to **inefficiencies, delays, and increased operational costs**.

Smartsheet automation helps manufacturers **streamline operations, enhance productivity, and improve accuracy** by:
- **Tracking production schedules** in real-time.
- **Automating inventory and supply chain management**.
- **Monitoring quality control and defect tracking**.
- **Ensuring compliance and safety reporting**.
- **Integrating with ERP and IoT systems** for seamless operations.

This chapter will explore how **Smartsheet automation can be leveraged to optimize production workflows, reduce downtime, and enhance overall efficiency** in manufacturing.

---

1. Key Challenges in Manufacturing Operations

- **Production delays** – Inefficient tracking of tasks and dependencies leads to bottlenecks.
- **Inventory shortages or overstocking** – Lack of real-time tracking causes supply chain issues.
- **Quality control issues** – Identifying defects manually slows response times.
- **Compliance risks** – Meeting industry regulations requires accurate documentation and reporting.
- **Lack of real-time visibility** – Delayed updates hinder decision-making.

By automating key processes with Smartsheet, manufacturers can reduce errors, speed up workflows, and optimize resource management.

---

2. Automating Production Scheduling and Tracking

Production schedules are **highly dynamic** and require constant adjustments based on demand, raw material availability, and machine capacity. Smartsheet helps **automate scheduling and track production progress in real-time**.

Steps to Automate Production Scheduling

1. **Create a Smartsheet Production Tracker**
   - Columns: **Job ID, Product Name, Assigned Team, Start Date, Due Date, Status, Completion %**
2. **Set up automated workflows:**
   - **Trigger:** When a new production order is added.
   - **Action:** Assign the task to the production team and notify them.
3. **Automate status updates:**
   - **Trigger:** When production reaches 50% completion.
   - **Action:** Update the **Status column** to "In Progress".
   - **Trigger:** When production reaches 100%, mark it as "Completed" and notify stakeholders.

Result: Real-time tracking of production ensures on-time delivery and reduces manual follow-ups.

---

3. Automating Inventory and Supply Chain Management

Efficient inventory management ensures that raw materials are available when needed **without overstocking** or causing supply shortages.

Example: Automating Inventory Restocking

1. **Trigger:** When inventory levels drop below a threshold.
2. **Action:**
   - Automatically generate a **purchase request** in Smartsheet.
   - Notify the **procurement team** to place an order.
   - If the item is out of stock from a preferred supplier, notify an alternate supplier.

🚀 **Result:** Inventory levels are maintained **proactively**, reducing downtime and production delays.

Example: Automating Supplier Performance Tracking

1. **Trigger:** When a new supplier order is placed.
2. **Action:** Track **delivery time, cost, and quality rating** for each supplier.
3. **Trigger:** If supplier delivery is late, send an **escalation alert** to procurement.

🚀 **Result:** Manufacturers can identify and **prioritize reliable suppliers**, improving supply chain efficiency.

---

4. Automating Quality Control and Defect Tracking

Maintaining **product quality** is critical in manufacturing. Smartsheet can automate **defect tracking, inspections, and compliance reporting**.

Example: Automating Defect Reporting and Resolution

1. **Trigger:** When a product defect is reported in Smartsheet.
2. **Action:**
   - Assign the defect to **the quality control team**.
   - Notify the **production manager** for review.
   - Update the defect resolution status as **"Pending Investigation"**.
3. **Trigger:** If the defect is unresolved within **48 hours**, send an **urgent alert** to management.

🚀 **Result:** Defects are tracked and resolved **efficiently**, preventing further production issues.

Example: Automating Compliance Audits

1. **Trigger:** When a compliance audit is due (based on predefined schedules).
2. **Action:**
   - Assign compliance tasks to relevant teams.
   - Generate a **compliance checklist** for inspectors.
   - Send automated reports to regulatory bodies.

🚀 **Result:** Compliance records are **automatically maintained**, reducing the risk of penalties.

---

5. Using Smartsheet Dashboards for Real-Time Manufacturing Insights

A **real-time manufacturing dashboard** provides managers with **live insights** into production, inventory, and quality control.

Steps to Create an Automated Manufacturing Dashboard

1. **Create a Smartsheet dashboard** with:
   - **Production progress metrics** (completed vs. pending tasks).
   - **Inventory levels** (real-time stock updates).
   - **Defect tracking summary** (open vs. resolved defects).
   - **Supplier performance ratings**.
2. **Automate dashboard updates:**
   - Connect Smartsheet data to the dashboard for **real-time updates**.
   - Send **weekly automated reports** to management.

🚀 **Result:** Decision-makers can **monitor operations in real time** and take action as needed.

---

6. Integrating Smartsheet with ERP and IoT Systems

Manufacturers use **ERP systems (SAP, Oracle, NetSuite)** and **IoT sensors** to manage operations. Smartsheet integrates with these systems to provide **a unified view of data**.

Example: Syncing Smartsheet with an ERP System

- **Trigger:** A new production order is created in the ERP system.
- **Action:** The order details are synced with Smartsheet, triggering **automated task assignments**.

Example: Using IoT Data for Automated Alerts

- **Trigger:** A **machine sensor detects a temperature spike** beyond safety limits.
- **Action:** An **urgent alert** is sent to the maintenance team in Smartsheet.

🚀 **Result:** Maintenance teams can **proactively address equipment issues**, reducing downtime.

---

7. Best Practices for Automating Manufacturing Workflows in Smartsheet

■ **Standardize production workflows** – Use templates to ensure consistent tracking.
■ **Automate repetitive tasks** – Reduce manual updates by setting automated triggers.
■ **Monitor real-time dashboards** – Ensure stakeholders have up-to-date insights.
■ **Integrate with ERP and IoT** – Sync Smartsheet with other manufacturing tools for efficiency.
■ **Review automation workflows regularly** – Optimize processes based on performance metrics.

Conclusion

Smartsheet automation enables manufacturers to **optimize production schedules, manage inventory efficiently, improve quality control, and enhance compliance tracking**. By integrating with **ERP systems and IoT data**, manufacturers can gain real-time insights into their operations and reduce manual workload.

Automating Financial Reporting and Budget Tracking

Financial reporting and budget tracking are **critical for organizations** to maintain financial health, monitor expenses, and ensure compliance. However, manually compiling financial data, tracking budgets, and generating reports can be time-consuming and prone to errors.

By leveraging **Smartsheet automation**, finance teams can:
- **Automate expense tracking** and approvals.
- **Generate financial reports dynamically** without manual updates.
- **Monitor budget performance** in real-time with dashboards.
- **Ensure compliance and audit readiness** through automated workflows.
- **Integrate Smartsheet with accounting tools** like QuickBooks, Xero, or NetSuite.

This chapter will guide you on **how to automate financial workflows in Smartsheet**, reducing manual work while improving accuracy and efficiency.

1. Challenges in Financial Reporting and Budget Tracking

Finance teams often struggle with:

- **Time-consuming manual reporting** – Collecting and consolidating data from multiple sources takes hours.
- **Delayed approvals** – Budget approvals and expense requests slow down decision-making.
- **Errors in financial data** – Manual data entry increases the risk of inaccuracies.
- **Lack of real-time visibility** – Finance teams need **live insights** into budget performance.
- **Compliance and audit issues** – Inconsistent financial record-keeping leads to compliance risks.

Smartsheet automation helps organizations overcome these challenges by standardizing financial workflows and automating reporting.

2. Automating Budget Tracking in Smartsheet

Tracking budgets in Smartsheet ensures **real-time visibility into financial performance** without the need for manual updates.

Steps to Automate Budget Tracking

1. **Create a Smartsheet Budget Tracker**
   - Columns: **Department, Expense Category, Budgeted Amount, Actual Spend, Variance, Approval Status**
2. **Set up automation rules:**
   - **Trigger:** When a new expense is logged.
   - **Action:** Compare the **actual spend vs. budgeted amount** and flag any overages.
3. **Send automatic alerts for budget overruns:**
   - **Trigger:** If actual spend exceeds 90% of the budget.
   - **Action:** Notify finance managers to review and adjust allocations.

Result: Finance teams get real-time alerts, preventing budget overruns.

3. Automating Expense Approval Workflows

Expense approvals can **delay projects and disrupt cash flow** if done manually. Smartsheet streamlines approvals through **automated workflows**.

Example: Automating Expense Approvals

1. **Trigger:** When an employee submits an expense request in Smartsheet.
2. **Condition:**
   o If **Amount < $1,000**, auto-approve the request.
   o If **Amount > $1,000**, send for manager approval.
3. **Action:**
   o Notify the manager via **email or Slack** for approval.
   o If approved, update status to **"Approved"** and notify Finance.
   o If rejected, update status to **"Revise & Resubmit"** and notify the requester.

🚀 **Result:** Expense approvals happen **faster**, reducing administrative burden.

---

4. Automating Financial Reporting and Dashboards

Finance teams rely on **regular reports** to analyze cash flow, spending, and revenue. Instead of manually compiling reports, Smartsheet **automates data consolidation and report generation**.

Steps to Automate Financial Reporting

1. **Create a financial reporting Smartsheet** with key metrics:
   o **Total Revenue, Expenses, Profit/Loss, Cash Flow, Accounts Payable & Receivable**
2. **Set up automated data consolidation:**
   o Use **cell linking** to pull data from different departments.
   o Automate updates based on real-time transactions.
3. **Schedule automated report delivery:**
   o **Trigger:** Every **Monday at 9 AM**.
   o **Action:** Generate a **weekly financial report** and send it to stakeholders.

🚀 **Result:** Finance teams **receive reports automatically**, reducing manual work.

Example: Creating an Automated Financial Dashboard

1. **Set up a Smartsheet dashboard** with:
   o **Real-time expense tracking** charts.
   o **Budget vs. actual spending** widgets.
   o **Profit and loss summary**.
   o **Forecasted cash flow projections**.
2. **Automate dashboard updates:**
   o Use Smartsheet reports to pull real-time financial data.
   o Schedule **weekly dashboard refreshes** for stakeholders.

🚀 **Result:** Management has **real-time visibility into financial health** without waiting for manual updates.

---

5. Integrating Smartsheet with Accounting and ERP Systems

Smartsheet can integrate with **accounting and ERP platforms** like:
■ **QuickBooks** – Sync financial data and automate invoice tracking.
■ **Xero** – Streamline expense reporting and reconciliation.
■ **NetSuite** – Automate budgeting and financial planning.

Example: Syncing Smartsheet with QuickBooks for Expense Tracking

- **Trigger:** A new expense is logged in Smartsheet.
- **Action:** Automatically create a **matching entry in QuickBooks**.
- **Result:** No need for **manual data entry**, reducing errors.

Example: Automating Payroll Approvals with NetSuite

- **Trigger:** Payroll entries are submitted in Smartsheet.
- **Action:** Sync with **NetSuite payroll system** for approval and processing.

🚀 **Result:** Payroll approvals happen **seamlessly**, reducing administrative workload.

---

6. Ensuring Compliance and Audit Readiness

Regulatory compliance requires **accurate and timely financial record-keeping**. Smartsheet can **automate compliance tracking and audit preparation**.

Example: Automating Financial Compliance Tracking

1. **Trigger:** A financial compliance audit is scheduled.
2. **Action:**
   - Assign audit tasks to **finance team members**.
   - Generate a **compliance checklist** for review.
   - Collect and store **required financial documents** automatically.

🚀 **Result:** Smartsheet ensures all compliance tasks are completed **before audit deadlines**.

---

7. Best Practices for Automating Financial Workflows in Smartsheet

■ **Standardize reporting templates** – Ensure all financial reports follow a consistent format.
■ **Automate approvals** – Reduce delays by using approval workflows for expenses and budgets.
■ **Integrate with accounting tools** – Sync Smartsheet with QuickBooks, Xero, or NetSuite.
■ **Use real-time dashboards** – Provide **live financial insights** to decision-makers.
■ **Monitor compliance metrics** – Automate audit preparation and regulatory tracking.

Conclusion

Smartsheet automation enables finance teams to **streamline budget tracking, accelerate approvals, and generate real-time financial reports**. By **integrating with accounting tools, automating dashboards, and ensuring compliance**, organizations can improve financial transparency and reduce manual effort.

Improving Customer Service with Automated Ticketing

Efficient customer service is essential for maintaining customer satisfaction and loyalty. However, **manual ticket management can be inefficient**, leading to delayed responses, unresolved issues, and frustrated customers.

By leveraging **Smartsheet automation**, organizations can:
- **Automate ticket creation and categorization**.
- **Assign tickets to the right team members** based on priority.
- **Send automated updates** to customers on issue status.
- **Track response times** and measure customer service performance.
- **Integrate Smartsheet with CRM and helpdesk software** (e.g., Zendesk, Freshdesk, or Salesforce).

This chapter will cover how to **set up an automated ticketing system in Smartsheet** to improve response times, streamline workflows, and enhance overall customer service.

---

1. Challenges in Customer Service Ticket Management

Common challenges in managing customer service tickets include:

- **Manual ticket sorting is time-consuming** – Customer issues come in from multiple channels (email, chat, phone), requiring manual organization.
- **Delayed responses and follow-ups** – Without automation, customers experience long wait times.
- **Inefficient issue escalation** – Critical issues may not be addressed promptly.
- **Lack of visibility into ticket status** – Customers and support teams struggle to track progress.
- **Difficulty in measuring service performance** – Managers lack real-time insights into response and resolution times.

Smartsheet automation ensures that every ticket is handled efficiently, reducing response times and improving service quality.

---

2. Automating Ticket Creation and Categorization

The first step in setting up an **automated ticketing system** is ensuring that all customer inquiries are captured, categorized, and assigned correctly.

Example: Automating Ticket Creation in Smartsheet

1. **Set up a Customer Service Ticket Tracker in Smartsheet**
   - Columns: **Ticket ID, Customer Name, Issue Category, Priority, Status, Assigned Agent, Created Date, Resolution Date**
2. **Create an automated intake form** using **Smartsheet Forms** to allow customers to submit tickets.
   - Include dropdowns for **Issue Category** (e.g., Technical Support, Billing, Account Access).
3. **Set up an automation rule:**
   - **Trigger:** When a new ticket is submitted via the form.
   - **Action:**
     - Categorize the ticket based on keywords.
     - Assign **urgent tickets to a senior agent** automatically.
     - Notify the **assigned agent and customer** via email.

🚀 Result: Tickets are automatically sorted and assigned, reducing manual sorting time.

---

3. Automating Ticket Assignments and Escalations

Assigning tickets **manually** can cause **delays**, especially for **high-priority issues**. Smartsheet can automatically assign tickets based on **priority, agent workload, or issue type**.

Example: Automatically Assigning Tickets Based on Priority

1. **Trigger:** When a ticket is submitted.
2. **Condition:**
   - If **Priority = "High"**, assign to **Senior Support Team**.
   - If **Priority = "Medium"**, assign to **General Support**.
   - If **Priority = "Low"**, assign to **Tier 1 Support**.
3. **Action:**
   - Notify the assigned agent with ticket details.
   - If the ticket is **not resolved in 24 hours**, escalate to **Support Manager**.

🚀 Result: High-priority issues are addressed first, improving response time and customer satisfaction.

---

4. Automating Customer Updates and Follow-Ups

Customers want to stay informed about their ticket status without repeatedly contacting support. Smartsheet can **automatically send updates** based on ticket progress.

Example: Sending Automatic Status Updates

1. **Trigger:** When a ticket **status changes** (e.g., "In Progress" → "Resolved").
2. **Action:**
   - Send an **email notification** to the customer with the updated status.
   - Provide a **feedback link** for the customer to rate the service.
   - If the customer **does not respond within 48 hours**, close the ticket automatically.

🚀 Result: Customers receive timely updates, improving transparency and satisfaction.

---

5. Tracking and Reporting Customer Service Performance

Measuring **customer service efficiency** is crucial for **continuous improvement**. Smartsheet can **automate the tracking of key performance indicators (KPIs)**.

Example: Creating a Customer Service Dashboard

1. **Create a Smartsheet dashboard** with:
   - **Average response time per agent**.
   - **Number of open vs. resolved tickets**.
   - **Customer satisfaction scores** (collected from automated feedback forms).
   - **Escalation trends** (how many tickets required manager intervention).
2. **Set up automated reports:**
   - **Trigger:** Every **Monday at 9 AM**.
   - **Action:** Generate a **weekly service report** and email it to support managers.

🚀 Result: Managers get real-time insights into **service performance**, helping improve response times.

6. Integrating Smartsheet with CRM and Helpdesk Software

Smartsheet can **connect with CRM and ticketing systems** to **streamline workflows** across multiple platforms.

- **Zendesk:** Sync ticket data between Smartsheet and Zendesk for unified tracking.
- **Salesforce:** Track customer interactions and service requests automatically.
- **Freshdesk:** Automate support ticket assignments between platforms.

Example: Syncing Smartsheet with Zendesk for Ticket Resolution

- **Trigger:** A **ticket is closed** in Smartsheet.
- **Action:** Update the **status in Zendesk**, closing the support request.
- **Result:** Customer data is **automatically synchronized**, eliminating manual data entry.

🚀 **Result:** Support teams **reduce duplication of effort**, improving response efficiency.

7. Best Practices for Automating Customer Service Workflows in Smartsheet

- **Use automation for ticket assignments** – Ensure urgent issues are prioritized automatically.
- **Automate customer follow-ups** – Keep customers informed of ticket status.
- **Integrate with CRM and helpdesk tools** – Reduce manual work by syncing Smartsheet with Zendesk, Salesforce, or Freshdesk.
- **Monitor service performance dashboards** – Track response times, resolution rates, and customer feedback.
- **Regularly optimize workflows** – Review and refine automation rules based on support team feedback.

Conclusion

Automating customer service ticketing in Smartsheet **reduces manual workload, speeds up response times, and enhances customer satisfaction**. By **automating ticket assignments, status updates, and performance tracking**, organizations can **deliver exceptional customer support with greater efficiency**.

Section 6:
Best Practices and Optimization

Designing Efficient Automation Workflows

Automation workflows in Smartsheet help **reduce manual effort, improve accuracy, and enhance team productivity**. However, **poorly designed automation** can create confusion, inefficiencies, and even workflow failures.

To ensure **efficiency and scalability**, it is essential to:
■ **Define clear objectives** for each automation.
■ **Use structured triggers, conditions, and actions** for smooth execution.
■ **Eliminate redundant steps** to enhance speed.
■ **Ensure data accuracy and security** within automated processes.
■ **Regularly review and optimize** workflows for continuous improvement.

This chapter explores **best practices for designing Smartsheet automation workflows**, ensuring they remain effective, scalable, and adaptable.

---

1. Key Principles of an Efficient Automation Workflow

A well-designed automation workflow should follow these principles:

* **Clarity** – Ensure that automation logic is **easy to understand** and maintain.
* **Scalability** – Design workflows that **work across teams and projects**.
* **Reliability** – Prevent automation **failures due to incorrect logic**.
* **Minimal manual intervention** – Reduce human dependency with **self-updating processes**.
* **Performance tracking** – Use Smartsheet reports to measure workflow effectiveness.

■ **By applying these principles, businesses can streamline operations without creating unnecessary complexity.**

---

2. Structuring an Effective Automation Workflow in Smartsheet

Each **Smartsheet automation** follows a structure:

1. Trigger → 2. Condition (if applicable) → 3. Action

Example: Automating Task Assignments for a Project

1. **Trigger:** When a **new project task** is added.
2. **Condition:** If **Task Priority = High**, assign it to a senior project manager.
3. **Action:**
   ○ Update the **Task Owner** column.
   ○ Send an **email notification** to the assigned user.

🚀 **Result:** Tasks are assigned **instantly** without manual intervention.

---

3. Choosing the Right Automation Triggers

Triggers **initiate automation** in Smartsheet. Selecting the right trigger ensures workflows run **at the correct time without unnecessary executions**.

Types of Triggers in Smartsheet:

■ **When a row is added or changed** – Useful for tracking **new entries or updates**.
■ **When a date is reached** – Automates **recurring tasks, reminders, and deadlines**.
■ **When a field value changes** – Ideal for **progress updates and approvals**.

Example: Automating Monthly Budget Reviews

- **Trigger:** When the **first day of each month arrives**.
- **Action:**
    - ○ Generate a **budget summary report**.
    - ○ Notify finance managers with an **automated email**.

🚀 **Result:** Finance teams receive reports **without manual data collection**.

---

4. Avoiding Redundant or Conflicting Automation

🔒 **Common Issues in Workflow Design:**
✖ **Duplicate automation rules** leading to multiple actions for the same event.
✖ **Conflicting conditions** where different automations override each other.
✖ **Too many triggers** slowing down Smartsheet performance.

Best Practices to Prevent Conflicts:

■ **Group similar automation rules** together.
■ **Use conditional logic** to avoid unnecessary automation triggers.
■ **Test automation in a sandbox** before applying it to live projects.

Example: Avoiding Redundant Email Notifications

Instead of **sending an email for every task update**, set a condition:
■ **Trigger:** When task status changes **to "Completed"**.
■ **Condition:** Send email **only if Assigned User ≠ "N/A"**.

🚀 **Result:** Only relevant users receive updates, reducing email overload.

---

5. Optimizing Workflows with Conditional Logic

Conditional logic ensures **automation adapts to different scenarios** instead of following a rigid process.

Example: Automating Leave Requests in HR

1. **Trigger:** When a **new leave request** is submitted.
2. **Condition:**
    - ○ If **leave is ≤ 3 days**, auto-approve.
    - ○ If **leave is > 3 days**, send for manager approval.
3. **Action:**
    - ○ Update request status to **"Approved" or "Pending"**.
    - ○ Notify HR and the employee.

🚀 **Result:** HR does not need to **manually process** every request.

---

6. Ensuring Data Accuracy and Security in Automation

Poorly managed automation can **introduce data errors** or **compromise security**.

■ **Use data validation rules** to prevent incorrect inputs.
■ **Restrict automation permissions** to limit unauthorized changes.
■ **Ensure sensitive workflows** (e.g., finance approvals) are encrypted or password-protected.

Example: Protecting Confidential Data in Financial Workflows

1. **Trigger:** When a new financial report is generated.
2. **Condition:** If **User Role = "Finance Manager"**, grant access.
3. **Action:** Notify only **authorized users** and **hide financial data from others**.

🚀 **Result:** Only relevant personnel can **view financial reports**, ensuring compliance.

---

7. Monitoring and Optimizing Automation Performance

Automation workflows should be **monitored and improved continuously**.

Key Metrics to Track in Smartsheet Dashboards

■ **Time saved** using automation vs. manual tasks.
■ **Error reduction rate** after workflow implementation.
■ **Number of automated approvals vs. manual approvals**.

Example: Reviewing Automation Efficiency for a Marketing Team

- **Trigger:** Generate an **automation performance report** every month.
- **Action:** Identify **underperforming automation** and optimize workflows.

🚀 **Result:** The marketing team refines workflows **based on data-driven insights**.

---

8. Best Practices for Designing Scalable Automation Workflows

■ **Start with simple workflows** – Test automation with basic triggers before adding complexity.
■ **Use a central automation tracker** – Document all Smartsheet automation rules to avoid conflicts.
■ **Automate frequently used tasks first** – Focus on high-impact processes like approvals, task assignments, and reporting.
■ **Review automation regularly** – Set a quarterly review process to optimize workflows.
■ **Test before deployment** – Run automation in **test sheets** before applying to live data.

Conclusion: Designing efficient Smartsheet automation workflows requires **clarity, logic, and continuous optimization**. By applying **best practices**, organizations can ensure their automation is **scalable, error-free, and aligned with business goals**.

Avoiding Common Automation Pitfalls

While Smartsheet automation can **significantly reduce manual effort and improve efficiency**, poorly designed workflows can lead to **errors, workflow breakdowns, and unintended consequences**.

Common **automation pitfalls** include:
✘ **Overcomplicating workflows** – Creating too many triggers and actions.
✘ **Ignoring workflow testing** – Failing to test automation before deployment.
✘ **Conflicting rules** – Automation rules overriding each other.
✘ **Lack of user permissions** – Automation failing due to restricted access.
✘ **Not reviewing performance** – Letting inefficient workflows run without optimization.

This chapter will explore **the most common automation mistakes** and provide **practical solutions** to ensure **error-free and effective automation** in Smartsheet.

---

1. Overcomplicating Automation Workflows

🪧 **Problem:**
Many users create **complex automation workflows** with too many triggers, conditions, and actions. This makes automation difficult to manage, troubleshoot, and scale.

⬛ **Solution:**
- **Keep automation simple** – Start with essential workflows and expand gradually.
- **Use multi-step workflows instead of separate rules** – Avoid cluttering automation settings.
- **Group similar automations** – Reduce redundancy by merging related tasks.

Example: Simplifying a Task Assignment Workflow

✘ **Overcomplicated:**

- Separate automations for each priority level (High, Medium, Low).
- Multiple triggers for new task creation, status updates, and escalations.

⬛ **Optimized Workflow:**

- **One automation rule:** If "Priority = High", assign to **Senior Manager**.
- **One conditional trigger:** If task is not updated in **48 hours**, send escalation.

🚀 **Result:** Fewer automations, easier troubleshooting, and a more efficient process.

---

2. Failing to Test Automation Before Deployment

🪧 **Problem:**
Many users **deploy automation directly into live projects**, leading to **unexpected errors** and disruption.

⬛ **Solution:**
- **Create a test Smartsheet** – Run automations in a sandbox environment before using them in real projects.
- **Use sample data** – Test workflows with mock entries to identify issues.
- **Manually execute workflows first** – Before automating a process, test it manually to confirm its logic.

Example: Testing a Recurring Task Automation

1. **Create a separate testing sheet** with **dummy data**.
2. **Run automation on test data** and check for expected outcomes.
3. **Monitor logs for errors** before applying to real projects.

✈ **Result:** Automation works **as expected** without disrupting live operations.

---

3. Conflicting or Redundant Automation Rules

🔋 **Problem:**
Creating multiple **automation rules for the same process** can cause conflicts, resulting in:
✗ **Duplicate actions (e.g., multiple emails sent for the same event)**.
✗ **One automation overriding another** (e.g., different assignments for the same task).

■ **Solution:**
- **Use a central automation tracker** – Maintain a document listing all Smartsheet automation rules.
- **Review automation dependencies** – Ensure different workflows don't conflict.
- **Test automation in batches** – Enable rules one at a time to monitor interactions.

Example: Preventing Duplicate Notifications

✗ **Problem:** Multiple workflows trigger emails when a task status changes.
■ **Fix:** Modify the condition so that:

- Email **only sends when Status = "In Progress"** for the first time.
- If the task is marked **"Completed"**, notifications stop.

✈ **Result:** Smartsheet sends **only one notification per status change**, reducing email clutter.

---

4. Not Setting Proper User Permissions

🔋 **Problem:**
Automations can **fail silently** if the user who created them **does not have the correct permissions** to execute the actions.

■ **Solution:**
- **Ensure automation owners have full access** – The creator of an automation must have permission to modify data.
- **Use Smartsheet Admin tools** – Assign **Automation Admins** to monitor and troubleshoot failures.
- **Test automation with different user roles** – Ensure workflows work for all required team members.

Example: Fixing an Automation Failure Due to Permissions

✗ **Problem:** An automation rule fails to assign tasks because the owner lacks edit permissions.
■ **Fix:**

1. Change the automation owner to a **Smartsheet Admin**.
2. Ensure **"Edit Access"** is enabled for all relevant users.
3. Run a **test assignment** to confirm the fix.

✈ **Result:** Automation runs **smoothly** without permission-related failures.

---

5. Not Reviewing and Optimizing Automation Performance

Problem:

Without regular monitoring, automation can:

✗ **Become outdated** – Processes change, but automation remains the same.

✗ **Cause inefficiencies** – Unoptimized workflows increase **execution time**.

✗ **Fail silently** – Errors can go unnoticed if automation is not reviewed.

Solution:

• **Set a quarterly automation review** – Ensure workflows are up to date.

• **Use Smartsheet dashboards to track automation metrics** – Monitor execution times and success rates.

• **Collect team feedback** – Regularly ask users if automation is improving workflow efficiency.

Example: Reviewing and Optimizing a Sales Automation Workflow

Metric to track:

- Number of automated lead follow-ups per month.
- Response rate from customers.
- Time saved compared to manual follow-ups.

🚀 **Result:** Automation continuously improves **based on data-driven insights**.

---

6. Not Using Conditional Logic for Smarter Automation

Problem:

Users often create **separate automations for different cases** instead of using **conditional logic** within one workflow.

Solution:

• **Combine conditions within one automation rule** instead of creating multiple workflows.

• **Use "If-Then" logic** to streamline decision-making.

• **Leverage formula-based triggers** for advanced automation.

Example: Smart Task Escalation with Conditional Logic

✗ **Inefficient Workflow:**

- Separate automation rules for **"High Priority"**, **"Medium Priority"**, and **"Low Priority"** tickets.

Optimized Workflow Using Conditional Logic:

1. **Trigger:** When a task status is updated.
2. **Condition:**
   ○ If **Priority = High**, escalate to the Senior Manager.
   ○ If **Priority = Medium**, escalate to Team Lead.
   ○ If **Priority = Low**, assign to general support.

🚀 **Result:** One workflow replaces multiple automation rules, improving efficiency.

---

7. Ignoring Security and Compliance Risks

Problem:

Without proper security measures, **automation can expose sensitive data** or **allow unauthorized access**.

■ Solution:
- **Restrict access to confidential sheets** – Use role-based permissions.
- **Automate audit logs** – Track who modifies automation workflows.
- **Set up approval workflows** for sensitive automation actions.

Example: Automating Financial Data Access Securely

1. **Trigger:** A finance report is generated.
2. **Condition:**
   - Only send the report if the user is in the **Finance Department**.
3. **Action:**
   - If authorized, email the report.
   - If unauthorized, log the access attempt.

🚀 **Result:** Financial data is **secure and accessible only to the right people**.

Conclusion

Avoiding automation pitfalls ensures Smartsheet workflows **run efficiently, securely, and without errors**. By following best practices such as **testing before deployment, using conditional logic, monitoring performance, and optimizing permissions**, organizations can **maximize automation benefits**.

Measuring the Impact of Automation on Productivity

Implementing automation in Smartsheet can **save time, reduce errors, and improve efficiency**—but how do you measure its actual impact on productivity? Without tracking performance, it's difficult to determine whether automation is truly delivering the expected benefits.

By measuring automation's impact, organizations can:
- **Quantify time saved compared to manual workflows.**
- **Evaluate efficiency improvements across teams and departments.**
- **Track key performance indicators (KPIs) related to workflow automation.**
- **Identify areas for further optimization and cost savings.**
- **Demonstrate the ROI (Return on Investment) of Smartsheet automation.**

This chapter will guide you through **key metrics, Smartsheet reports, and best practices** to measure and maximize the impact of automation.

---

1. Key Metrics for Measuring Automation Success

To assess how automation affects productivity, track the following **key performance indicators (KPIs):**

- **Time Savings Per Task** – Compare time spent on tasks before and after automation.
- **Reduction in Manual Data Entry** – Measure the decrease in human input required.
- **Task Completion Speed** – Track how much faster tasks are completed.
- **Workflow Efficiency** – Analyze the number of steps eliminated through automation.
- **Error Reduction** – Measure decreases in data entry errors or missed deadlines.
- **Automation Execution Rate** – Track how often automation rules successfully run.

By tracking these metrics, teams can determine whether automation is **improving productivity and streamlining processes effectively**.

---

2. Using Smartsheet Reports to Track Automation Efficiency

Smartsheet **provides built-in reporting and dashboards** that allow users to visualize and analyze automation performance.

Example: Creating an Automation Impact Report

1. **Set up a Smartsheet report** that includes:
   - Task Name, Start Time, Completion Time, Assigned User, Automation Type.
2. **Use calculated fields** to measure:
   - Time saved per task (Before vs. After Automation).
   - Error rate (Number of issues reported before and after automation).
3. **Generate a monthly report** to track improvements over time.

🚀 **Result:** Teams can identify which automation workflows are delivering the most value.

---

3. Comparing Manual vs. Automated Workflows

To demonstrate the impact of automation, compare **manual workflows before automation** with **automated workflows after implementation**.

Example: Measuring Time Savings in Task Approvals

📌 **Before Automation:**

- Task approvals took **48 hours** on average due to manual follow-ups.
  📌 **After Automation:**
- Automated approvals reduced response time to **6 hours**.

⬛ **Productivity Gain: 87.5% reduction in approval time!**

By documenting improvements in **task speed, accuracy, and efficiency**, teams can validate the effectiveness of automation.

---

4. Using Dashboards to Visualize Automation Performance

Dashboards in Smartsheet provide a **real-time view** of automation performance, helping teams track progress and identify bottlenecks.

How to Build an Automation Dashboard in Smartsheet

1. **Add widgets displaying:**
    - ⬛ Total tasks automated per month
    - ⏳ Average task completion time (Before vs. After automation)
    - ⚡ Number of automation runs per workflow
    - ⬛ Error reduction rate
2. **Use color-coded charts** to identify improvements.

🚀 **Result:** Stakeholders can quickly assess automation performance **at a glance**.

---

5. Assessing the ROI (Return on Investment) of Automation

To determine whether Smartsheet automation is delivering financial value, calculate **the Return on Investment (ROI)**:

ROI Formula:

ROI = [(Time & Cost Savings from Automation - Implementation Costs) / Implementation Costs] × 100

Example ROI Calculation:

- **Before Automation:** Employees spent **20 hours per week** on manual data entry.
- **After Automation:** Workload was reduced to **3 hours per week**.
- **Annual Savings:** 17 hours/week × 52 weeks = **884 hours saved per year**.
- **Cost Savings:** If an employee's hourly wage is **$30**, savings amount to **$26,520 annually**.

🚀 **Result:** Automation is saving significant time and resources, justifying the investment in Smartsheet automation.

---

6. Identifying Bottlenecks and Further Optimization Opportunities

Even after implementing automation, **ongoing optimization** ensures continued efficiency gains.

🔍 **Regularly review reports to identify:**

- Automations that **fail frequently** or do not run as expected.
- Workflows that **still require manual intervention** and could be automated.
- Tasks that **are taking longer than expected**, indicating inefficiencies.

Example: Optimizing an Underperforming Workflow

🔔 **Issue:** An automation rule for expense approvals **frequently fails** because requests exceed predefined budget limits.
■ **Fix:** Adjust the workflow to **escalate high-value requests** to a finance manager instead of failing.

🚀 **Result:** The process is now **fully automated without disruptions**.

---

7. Best Practices for Tracking Automation Success

■ **Set automation benchmarks** – Define baseline metrics before automation implementation.
■ **Review automation logs** – Regularly check Smartsheet's execution history to catch issues early.
■ **Use user feedback** – Ask employees if automation is improving their productivity.
■ **Continuously refine workflows** – Update automation rules as business processes evolve.
■ **Monitor cost vs. benefits** – Ensure automation delivers measurable savings.

Conclusion

Measuring the impact of automation in Smartsheet allows organizations to **quantify efficiency gains, track productivity improvements, and demonstrate ROI**. By **using reports, dashboards, and performance tracking**, teams can continuously refine workflows to maximize automation benefits.

Scaling Automation Across Teams and Departments

Automating workflows at an individual or team level provides significant productivity gains, but the **true power of automation** is realized when it is **scaled across entire departments and organizations**. Scaling automation ensures **consistent processes, improved collaboration, and maximum efficiency** across multiple teams.

In this chapter, we will cover:
■ **The benefits of scaling automation** across teams.
■ **Key considerations before expanding automation** beyond single teams.
■ **Best practices for implementing company-wide automation.**
■ **Overcoming challenges** when scaling Smartsheet automation.

1. Why Scale Automation Across Teams?

Expanding Smartsheet automation from one team to multiple departments brings several advantages:

📌 **Standardization of Processes:** Consistent workflows ensure uniformity in task execution and approvals.
📌 **Reduced Operational Overhead:** Automating repetitive tasks at scale saves time and effort.
📌 **Faster Decision-Making:** Automated reporting and notifications keep key stakeholders informed.
📌 **Seamless Collaboration:** Workflows integrate multiple teams, improving coordination.
📌 **Scalability and Flexibility:** Automation can adapt as business needs grow.

🚀 **Result:** A **smarter, more agile organization** that leverages automation for operational excellence.

2. Key Considerations Before Scaling Automation

Before expanding automation across multiple teams, consider the following:

◆ **Identify High-Impact Workflows:** Prioritize automations that **benefit multiple departments**, such as finance approvals, HR onboarding, or IT support requests.
◆ **Ensure Workflow Compatibility:** Different teams may have **unique requirements**—customize automation to fit their needs.
◆ **Assign Ownership and Permissions:** Define **who controls automation rules** and manage access levels to prevent conflicts.
◆ **Train Teams on Automation Best Practices:** Employees should **understand how automation works** to maximize efficiency.
◆ **Establish Monitoring & Reporting:** Track **performance metrics** to measure automation success and identify improvements.

🚀 **Result:** A **smooth transition** from isolated automation to a **company-wide system**.

3. Best Practices for Implementing Company-Wide Automation

A. Standardizing Automation Workflows Across Teams

Consistency is key when scaling automation. Ensure teams follow **a unified approach** to avoid redundancy and errors.

■ **Create a Centralized Automation Library** – Maintain a **repository of Smartsheet automation templates** for common tasks.
■ **Use Standard Naming Conventions** – Ensure workflows are **clearly labeled** (e.g., "HR_Onboarding_Approval" vs. "Random_Workflow_1").
■ **Define Universal Rules & Guidelines** – Establish **company-wide best practices** for automation usage.

🚀 **Result: Easier collaboration and troubleshooting** across teams.

B. Leveraging Cross-Team Workflow Automation

Some processes **span multiple departments**—such as project approvals, budget tracking, or customer service workflows. Use **automated handoffs** between teams to streamline operations.

Example: Automating a Multi-Departmental Expense Approval Process

1 **Employee submits an expense request (HR).**
2 **Finance team reviews the request and verifies budget.**
3 **Approval is sent to senior management.**
4 **Approved expenses are processed by the accounting team.**

- **Without Automation:** Email chains cause **delays and confusion**.
- **With Smartsheet Automation:** Tasks are **instantly routed** to the right department with **automated approvals and notifications**.

🚀 **Result: Faster processing, fewer delays, and complete transparency.**

C. Implementing Role-Based Automation Access

Different teams require **different automation permissions** to prevent unauthorized modifications.

📌 **Best Practices for Automation Access Management:**
- **Use Role-Based Permissions:** Assign **view, edit, or admin access** based on team roles.
- **Restrict High-Security Workflows:** Financial or HR automation should be **limited to authorized personnel**.
- **Allow Teams to Customize, Not Modify Core Automation:** Standard workflows should **remain unchanged**, while teams can **add department-specific tweaks**.

🚀 **Result: Secure, controlled automation workflows** with minimal risk.

---

4. Overcoming Challenges in Scaling Automation

🔔 **Challenge 1: Resistance to Change**
Some employees may **hesitate to adopt automation**, fearing **job displacement** or **workflow disruptions**.

■ **Solution:**
- Educate teams on **how automation enhances productivity** rather than replacing jobs.
- Offer **training sessions** to help employees understand automation tools.
- Demonstrate **real-world benefits** using case studies.

🚀 **Result: Increased employee buy-in and smoother adoption** of automation.

Challenge 2: Automation Failures at Scale
More automation = **higher complexity**, leading to **potential errors or conflicts**.

Solution:
- **Regularly audit automation rules** to eliminate redundant or conflicting workflows.
- **Test automations in a pilot environment** before deploying them organization-wide.
- **Monitor execution logs** to quickly identify failures.

Result: Reliable automation that scales smoothly.

Challenge 3: Maintaining Automation Consistency Across Teams
Without standardization, teams might **set up inconsistent workflows** that cause **data mismatches**.

Solution:
- **Use standardized templates** for workflows across departments.
- **Hold quarterly automation reviews** to ensure consistency.
- **Designate an Automation Admin** to oversee organization-wide Smartsheet workflows.

Result: Unified automation that maintains data integrity.

---

5. Measuring the Success of Scaled Automation

To ensure automation is effective at an enterprise level, track **key performance indicators (KPIs)**:

Time Savings Per Workflow: Compare **pre- and post-automation task duration**.
Error Reduction Rate: Measure **decreased manual input errors**.
Process Completion Speed: Track how much **faster approvals and tasks are completed**.
Employee Productivity Gains: Monitor how many **work hours were saved through automation**.
Adoption Rate: Check how many **teams actively use automation**.

Example: Measuring the Impact of Scaling Automation

Before Scaling: 3 teams using automation, **saving 10 hours/week per team**.
After Scaling: 10 teams using automation, **saving 100+ hours/week company-wide**.

Conclusion: Scaling automation **massively increases efficiency and reduces operational costs**.

Conclusion

Scaling Smartsheet automation across teams and departments leads to **standardized, efficient, and collaborative workflows**. By **following best practices, addressing challenges, and tracking KPIs**, organizations can maximize automation benefits **at an enterprise level**.

Maintaining Security and Compliance in Automated Processes

As organizations adopt **Smartsheet automation**, ensuring **data security, user permissions, and regulatory compliance** becomes essential. Automation processes can involve **sensitive information**, such as **financial records, employee data, and customer details**, making it critical to implement **robust security measures**.

In this chapter, we'll cover:
- **Key security risks in automation** and how to mitigate them.
- **Best practices for secure automation workflows** in Smartsheet.
- **Ensuring compliance with industry regulations and data protection laws.**

---

1. Understanding Security Risks in Automation

While automation enhances efficiency, it also introduces **security vulnerabilities** if not configured correctly. Some common risks include:

- **Unauthorized Access** – Users without proper permissions may gain access to confidential data.
- **Data Leaks & Breaches** – Automated workflows sending data to unintended recipients.
- **Misconfigured Permissions** – Automation rules executing actions beyond user privileges.
- **Lack of Audit Trails** – No record of who accessed or modified workflows.

Solution: Implement **role-based access, encryption, and logging** to prevent security breaches.

---

2. Best Practices for Securing Smartsheet Automation

To maintain security and compliance, organizations should follow **industry-standard security measures** when configuring Smartsheet automation.

A. Enforcing Role-Based Access Controls (RBAC)

Access control ensures that only **authorized users** can create, modify, or execute automation workflows.

📌 **Steps to Implement RBAC in Smartsheet:**

1. **Limit Automation Ownership:** Assign automation management to **trusted admins only**.
2. **Use Group-Based Permissions:** Assign automation access based on **roles or departments**.
3. **Restrict Data Editing Rights:** Ensure only relevant team members can modify workflow rules.

🚀 **Result:** Prevents **unauthorized modifications** and enhances security.

B. Implementing Secure Data Handling in Automated Workflows

Automation workflows often handle **sensitive business data**. Use **secure handling methods** to prevent leaks.

📌 **Best Practices for Secure Data Handling:**
- **Avoid Sending Sensitive Data via Email Automation** – Instead, use **restricted dashboards or shared sheets**.
- **Use Data Masking for Confidential Fields** – Hide or encrypt fields like passwords or financial data.

■ **Implement Approval Workflows** – Add manual approval steps before processing **highly sensitive information**.

✈ **Result:** Prevents **accidental data exposure** through automated actions.

C. Configuring Audit Logs and Monitoring Automation Activities

■ **Why it's important:** Logs **track all automation executions**, helping teams **detect suspicious activity**.

📌 **How to Set Up Logging & Monitoring in Smartsheet:**
■ **Enable Activity Logs** – Keep records of all automation triggers and modifications.
■ **Use Smartsheet Reports to Track Changes** – Maintain **automated change logs** to detect anomalies.
■ **Review Logs Periodically** – Conduct **quarterly audits** to identify security vulnerabilities.

✈ **Result:** Maintains **transparency and accountability** in automation execution.

D. Securing Integrations with Third-Party Apps (Zapier, Microsoft Teams, Slack, etc.)

Many organizations **connect Smartsheet automation** with external tools like **Zapier, Teams, and Slack**. Improper configurations can expose sensitive data.

📌 **Best Practices for Secure Integrations:**
■ **Restrict API Access to Trusted Users Only** – Limit who can connect Smartsheet to external services.
■ **Use API Keys and OAuth Authentication** – Protect automation APIs with **secure authentication**.
■ **Audit Third-Party Integrations Regularly** – Disable **unused or outdated connections**.

✈ **Result:** Ensures **secure data exchange** with external platforms.

---

3. Ensuring Compliance with Industry Regulations

Organizations must **align automation workflows** with compliance frameworks such as **GDPR, HIPAA, SOC 2, and ISO 27001**.

A. GDPR (General Data Protection Regulation) Compliance

📌 **Key Requirements:**

- **Data Minimization:** Automate only **necessary** data processing tasks.
- **Access Controls:** Ensure only **authorized employees** access personal data.
- **Right to Erasure:** Enable **data deletion automation** when required.

✈ **Best Practice:** Use **Smartsheet forms and approval workflows** to document **user consent** before processing personal data.

B. HIPAA (Health Insurance Portability and Accountability Act) Compliance

📌 **Key Requirements for Healthcare Organizations Using Smartsheet:**

- **Encrypt Patient Data:** Do not expose **protected health information (PHI)** in automation workflows.
- **Audit Logs:** Maintain **detailed records** of automation execution and data access.
- **Access Controls:** Ensure **only healthcare professionals** access sensitive records.

🚀 **Best Practice:** Use **HIPAA-compliant cloud storage** for medical data and configure Smartsheet automation to **encrypt sensitive fields**.

C. SOC 2 and ISO 27001 Compliance for Enterprises

📌 **Best Practices for Compliance with Security Standards:**

- **Monitor Automation Execution Logs:** Keep a **detailed history** of all workflow changes.
- **Limit External Data Transfers:** Prevent automation from **sending sensitive data outside the organization**.
- **Use Secure File Storage:** Store confidential documents in **access-restricted Smartsheet attachments**.

🚀 **Best Practice:** Conduct **regular security audits** on Smartsheet workflows to maintain **SOC 2 and ISO 27001 compliance**.

---

4. How to Prevent Automation Failures that Compromise Security

Even with security controls, automation failures can **expose data or disrupt workflows**. Prevent security risks by:

📌 **Implementing Automation Fail-Safes:**
⬛ **Error Notifications:** Set up alerts for **failed automation runs**.
⬛ **Backup Automations:** Have **fallback rules** in case primary workflows fail.
⬛ **Testing Workflows Before Deployment:** Use **test environments** before launching **company-wide automation**.

🚀 **Result:** Prevents automation-related **security incidents and workflow disruptions**.

---

5. Reviewing and Updating Security Policies for Automation

Security threats evolve over time, making **ongoing reviews essential**.

📌 **Best Practices for Continuous Security Review:**
⬛ **Conduct Quarterly Security Audits** – Check for **automation misconfigurations** and **inactive workflows**.
⬛ **Update Role-Based Permissions Regularly** – Remove access for **former employees or inactive users**.
⬛ **Educate Employees on Security Awareness** – Train teams to **avoid automation misuse**.

🚀 **Result:** Keeps **automation workflows safe, secure, and compliant**.

Conclusion

Security and compliance in Smartsheet automation **protect sensitive data, prevent unauthorized access, and ensure regulatory adherence**. By **implementing role-based access controls, monitoring automation logs, securing integrations, and aligning workflows with compliance standards**, organizations can **scale automation safely and effectively**.

Section 7:
Troubleshooting and Support

Resolving Common Automation Errors

Smartsheet automation is a powerful tool, but **errors and unexpected failures** can sometimes disrupt workflows. Understanding **common automation issues, their causes, and troubleshooting techniques** ensures smooth operation and **maximizes efficiency**.

This chapter will cover:
- **Common automation errors and their causes**
- **Step-by-step troubleshooting methods**
- **Best practices for preventing automation failures**

1. Understanding Common Smartsheet Automation Errors

Error 1: Automation Rule Not Triggering
- **Cause:**

  - The trigger conditions **do not match** the data input.
  - The automation workflow is **disabled** or incorrectly configured.
  - The user making the change **lacks the required permissions**.

Solution:

  - Verify **trigger conditions** to ensure they align with expected inputs.
  - Check if the automation is **enabled** under the "Automation" tab.
  - Confirm the **user making changes** has sufficient permissions.

Error 2: Automation Running but Not Updating Data
- **Cause:**

  - The **target cell or column is locked** or restricted.
  - The workflow action is **not properly mapped** to the correct sheet.
  - The automation rule conflicts with **another rule or formula**.

Solution:

  - Unlock **protected cells** that automation needs to update.
  - Double-check **mapping settings** for accuracy.
  - Look for **overlapping automations** that might override each other.

Error 3: Approval Workflow Not Sending Notifications
- **Cause:**

- Email notifications are **disabled in Smartsheet settings**.
- The approver is **not assigned correctly** in the automation rule.
- The email is **filtered as spam** by the recipient's mail system.

Solution:

- Go to **User Profile > Notifications** and ensure emails are enabled.
- Confirm the **correct user or role** is assigned for approvals.
- Ask recipients to **whitelist Smartsheet emails** in their inbox.

Error 4: Delayed or Incomplete Automation Execution
- **Cause:**

- High Smartsheet **server load** causing execution lag.
- The automation depends on **external integrations (Zapier, API, etc.)** that have failed.
- Workflow **complexity** slowing down execution.

Solution:

- Wait and **retry the workflow** after a few minutes.
- Check the **status of third-party integrations** connected to Smartsheet.
- Simplify **complex workflows** by breaking them into **smaller automation rules**.

Error 5: Automation Stuck in a Loop or Running Multiple Times
- **Cause:**

- An automation rule is **triggering itself repeatedly** due to circular logic.
- Two or more workflows are **modifying the same data simultaneously**.

Solution:

- Add **filters or conditional logic** to **stop infinite loops**.
- Review **dependent automation rules** to prevent conflicting actions.

---

2. Step-by-Step Troubleshooting Guide

When facing automation errors, follow this **structured approach** to identify and fix the issue:

Step 1: Check the Automation Execution Log

Smartsheet provides an **activity log** for automation. Navigate to:
📌 **Automation > Manage Workflows > Execution Log**

Look for **warnings, skipped actions, or failed runs** to pinpoint errors.

Step 2: Verify Trigger Conditions

Many automation failures occur due to **incorrect trigger settings**.

■ Ensure the trigger **matches the actual data changes**.
■ If using **date-based triggers**, confirm the **date format is correct**.
■ Adjust **filter conditions** to capture **all relevant data inputs**.

Step 3: Test the Automation with a Sample Data Entry

■ Manually enter test data to **trigger the workflow** and observe its behavior.
■ If the automation **fails again**, review the logs to find discrepancies.

Step 4: Check User Permissions & Data Access

Some automations require **specific access levels** to function properly.

■ Ensure users modifying data have **Edit or Admin access** to the sheet.
■ If automation affects **multiple sheets**, confirm **cross-sheet permissions** are enabled.

Step 5: Look for Conflicting Rules or Formulas

If automation updates **calculated fields**, it may conflict with existing formulas.

■ Check if Smartsheet displays an **"Invalid Data Entry" warning**.
■ Move formulas to **separate reference columns** to avoid automation interference.

---

3. Best Practices for Preventing Automation Failures

✈ **1. Use Descriptive Workflow Names**
✗ Avoid: "Task Update 1"
■ Use: "Auto-Assign Task When Status = In Progress"

✈ **2. Keep Automation Workflows Simple & Modular**
📌 Instead of one **complex workflow**, break it into **smaller, linked automations**.

✈ **3. Regularly Review & Update Automation Rules**
📌 **Quarterly automation audits** help identify outdated or unnecessary rules.

✈ **4. Test New Automations in a Separate Smartsheet Before Deployment**
📌 Create a **test version** of your workflow and **validate its behavior** before applying it to live projects.

✈ **5. Enable Notifications for Automation Failures**
📌 Set up alerts to notify **admins when automation fails** to act quickly.

Conclusion

By understanding **common Smartsheet automation errors** and **applying structured troubleshooting techniques**, teams can **maintain error-free workflows and maximize efficiency**. Following **best practices** helps prevent failures, ensuring **reliable and scalable automation**.

Debugging Formula and Workflow Issues

Formulas and workflow automation are **powerful features in Smartsheet**, but errors can **disrupt workflows, cause incorrect data calculations, or result in unexpected behaviors**. Understanding how to **identify, troubleshoot, and fix** these issues will help you maintain **efficient and error-free automation processes**.

In this chapter, we'll cover:
- **Common formula-related errors and how to fix them**
- **Troubleshooting Smartsheet automation workflow issues**
- **Best practices for debugging formulas and workflows**

---

1. Common Formula Errors and How to Fix Them

Error 1: #INVALID DATA TYPE

• **Cause:** This error appears when a formula **expects a different type of data** than what is provided (e.g., a number instead of text).

Solution:

- Check **cell formatting** to ensure data types match.
- Use **VALUE()** to convert text numbers into actual numbers.
- If working with **dates**, use **DATE() or DATEVALUE()** to standardize formatting.

Error 2: #CIRCULAR REFERENCE

• **Cause:** A formula refers to **its own cell**, creating an endless loop.

Solution:

- Remove **self-referencing formulas** and break calculations into **separate columns**.
- Use **helper columns** for calculations that reference each other.

Error 3: #UNPARSEABLE

• **Cause:** Smartsheet **doesn't recognize the formula** due to:

- **Incorrect syntax**
- **Missing parentheses or commas**
- **Incorrect function names**

Solution:

- Use **Insert Function** in Smartsheet to check proper syntax.
- Ensure all **parentheses and quotation marks** are correctly placed.
- Cross-check **function spelling** and **arguments**.

Error 4: Formula Not Updating Automatically

- ◆ **Cause:** The sheet contains **locked columns, filters, or automation rules** that prevent updates.

■ **Solution:**

- Check if the column is **locked** and **unlock it if needed**.
- Ensure **filters are not hiding necessary data**.
- If using an **automation rule to modify cells**, ensure the automation **does not override manual formulas**.

2. Troubleshooting Workflow Automation Issues

Automation workflows can sometimes **fail to trigger, execute incorrectly, or behave unexpectedly**. Here's how to fix common issues:

■ Error 5: Workflow Not Triggering

- ◆ **Cause:**

- The trigger conditions **don't match** the actual data updates.
- The automation is **disabled** or hasn't been saved.
- The user **making changes lacks the necessary permissions**.

■ **Solution:**

- Double-check **workflow trigger conditions** to ensure they align with expected inputs.
- Navigate to **Automation > Manage Workflows** and verify if the rule is **enabled**.
- Ensure the user **triggering the change** has the **required access level**.

■ Error 6: Workflow Running but Not Performing the Expected Action

- ◆ **Cause:**

- The **target column is locked** or **not editable**.
- The workflow **modifies the wrong row or sheet**.
- Conflicts exist between **multiple automation rules** affecting the same data.

■ **Solution:**

- **Unlock** the necessary columns before running automation.
- Check **automation settings** to ensure they reference the correct **target sheet and column**.
- Review other **active workflows** to identify conflicting rules.

■ Error 7: Delayed or Skipped Automation Execution

- ◆ **Cause:**

- High **Smartsheet server load** during peak hours.
- The automation **depends on external tools (Zapier, API, etc.)**, which may be experiencing issues.
- The workflow has **too many conditional steps**, slowing execution.

■ **Solution:**

- Wait and **retry** after some time.
- Check the **status of external integrations** to ensure they are running properly.
- **Simplify** the workflow by **reducing the number of conditional steps**.

🔔 Error 8: Automation Overwriting or Deleting Data Unexpectedly

- ◆ **Cause:**

  - A workflow **modifies the wrong column or sheet** due to incorrect setup.
  - Automation **runs multiple times** because of overlapping rules.
  - The rule applies to **all rows instead of specific ones**.

- ■ **Solution:**

  - Add **filters and conditions** to automation rules to **target only relevant data**.
  - Adjust **execution frequency** to **prevent duplicate runs**.
  - Use the **"Only Trigger Once per Row"** option if the workflow **should not repeat for the same row**.

---

3. Step-by-Step Debugging Guide

Follow these steps when troubleshooting Smartsheet formula or workflow issues:

🔍 Step 1: Check for Errors in the Execution Log

📌 Navigate to **Automation > Manage Workflows > Execution Log** to check for **failed runs or skipped actions**.

■ If an error appears, adjust the **trigger conditions, permissions, or actions** accordingly.

🔍 Step 2: Test with Sample Data

■ Enter **test data** that meets the automation trigger conditions and observe whether the workflow runs correctly.

■ If using formulas, **try a different set of input values** to identify inconsistencies.

🔍 Step 3: Review Sheet Permissions & Access

📌 If an automation workflow **isn't updating data**, check **column permissions** and ensure **users have editing rights**.

■ If using **cross-sheet automation**, ensure the target sheet **allows external changes**.

🔍 Step 4: Use Helper Columns for Debugging

📌 Create **temporary columns** to test formulas or store **intermediate results** before finalizing automation rules.

■ This helps identify if **errors occur at a specific stage** in the process.

🔍 Step 5: Cross-Check Automation Rules

📌 Open **Automation > Manage Workflows** and **review all automation rules** to check for conflicts.

■ Deactivate **overlapping workflows** temporarily to test if an issue persists.

---

4. Best Practices for Preventing Formula and Workflow Errors

🚀 1. Keep Formulas Simple
📌 Break **complex formulas** into **smaller, modular expressions** for easier debugging.

🚀 2. Use Descriptive Names for Automation Workflows
✖ Avoid: "Task Rule 1"
■ Use: "Send Reminder When Due Date is 3 Days Away"

🚀 3. Regularly Test and Review Automation Rules
📌 Perform **quarterly reviews** of workflows to ensure they still **align with business needs**.

🚀 4. Document Workflow Rules and Dependencies
📌 Maintain a **log of automation rules, dependencies, and expected behaviors**.

🚀 5. Set Up Notification Alerts for Automation Failures
📌 Enable alerts to notify **admins when automation fails**, allowing for **quick resolution**.

Conclusion

By understanding **common formula and workflow issues** and applying structured **debugging techniques**, teams can ensure that **Smartsheet automation runs efficiently and without errors**.

Accessing Smartsheet's Knowledge Base and Community

Smartsheet provides a **comprehensive Knowledge Base and an active Community Forum** where users can find **troubleshooting guides, best practices, and expert advice**. Whether you're facing automation issues, formula errors, or simply looking to expand your skills, these resources are **invaluable for problem-solving and learning**.

This chapter will cover:
- **How to access Smartsheet's Knowledge Base**
- **Navigating the Smartsheet Community Forum**
- **Utilizing webinars, tutorials, and support resources**

1. Smartsheet Knowledge Base: Your First Stop for Help

The **Smartsheet Knowledge Base** (KB) is a **repository of guides, FAQs, and best practices** covering every aspect of Smartsheet, including:

- 📌 **Step-by-step automation tutorials**
- 📌 **Formula troubleshooting guides**
- 📌 **Integration setup walkthroughs**
- 📌 **Best practices for Smartsheet users**

🔍 How to Access the Knowledge Base

1. **Go to:** [Smartsheet Help Center] (https://help.smartsheet.com)
2. **Use the search bar** to enter keywords (e.g., "automation error," "workflow issues").
3. Click on **articles, video tutorials, or FAQs** to find solutions.

Pro Tip: Bookmark pages related to **automation, integrations, and troubleshooting** for quick access later.

2. Navigating the Smartsheet Community Forum

The **Smartsheet Community Forum** is an **interactive space** where users share **real-world experiences, solutions, and best practices**. It's a great place to:

- **Ask questions and get answers** from other Smartsheet users.
- **Search for discussions** on automation, formulas, and integrations.
- **Stay updated** with the latest feature releases and use cases.

🔍 How to Access the Community Forum

1. **Go to:** [Smartsheet Community] (https://community.smartsheet.com)
2. **Create a free account** (if you haven't already).
3. **Search or post a question** about your issue.
4. Engage with **Smartsheet experts and power users** to find solutions.

Pro Tip: Follow threads related to **automation and workflows** to stay updated on **troubleshooting strategies and new features**.

3. Smartsheet Webinars, Tutorials, and Training Resources

🎥 On-Demand Webinars & Video Tutorials

Smartsheet offers **free video tutorials and training sessions** covering **automation, formulas, integrations, and best practices**.

📌 Where to Find Webinars & Tutorials:

- **Smartsheet Help Center** ([https://help.smartsheet.com] (https://help.smartsheet.com))
- **Smartsheet YouTube Channel** ([https://www.youtube.com/user/Smartsheet] (https://www.youtube.com/user/Smartsheet))

⬛ **Pro Tip:** Watch Smartsheet's **"Automation Deep Dives"** for expert-level workflow optimization techniques.

🎓 Smartsheet University: Certification & Advanced Learning

Smartsheet University offers **structured courses and certifications** for those looking to become **power users**.

📌 **Available Courses:**
⬛ **Fundamentals of Smartsheet**
⬛ **Automation & Workflows**
⬛ **Advanced Formulas & Functions**
⬛ **Smartsheet API & Integrations**

🔍 **Access Smartsheet University:** [https://smartu.smartsheet.com] (https://smartu.smartsheet.com)

⬛ **Pro Tip:** Completing Smartsheet certification **boosts expertise** and makes automation **more effective**.

---

4. Using Smartsheet Support for Complex Issues

If the Knowledge Base and Community Forum don't resolve your issue, **contacting Smartsheet Support** is the next step.

🔍 How to Access Smartsheet Support

1️⃣ **Go to:** [Smartsheet Support Center] (https://www.smartsheet.com/contact)
2️⃣ Select the relevant support option:
📌 **Live Chat (for quick answers)**
📌 **Email Support (for complex issues)**
📌 **Phone Support (for priority users)**

⬛ **Pro Tip:** Before contacting support, **gather screenshots, error messages, and workflow details** to speed up resolution.

Conclusion

Smartsheet's **Knowledge Base, Community Forum, and training resources** are essential for **troubleshooting and improving automation skills**. By leveraging these resources, users can **quickly resolve automation issues, master Smartsheet's features, and stay updated on best practices**.

Contacting Smartsheet Support for Advanced Help

Even with Smartsheet's **automation tools and troubleshooting resources**, there may be times when you encounter **complex automation errors, API integration issues, or workflow failures** that require **direct assistance from Smartsheet's support team**.

This chapter will guide you through:
■ **How to access Smartsheet Support**
■ **The different support options available**
■ **Best practices for getting faster and more effective assistance**

1. When to Contact Smartsheet Support

Before reaching out to support, it's important to **determine whether your issue requires direct assistance**.

📌 **Common reasons to contact Smartsheet Support:**
■ **Automation rules not triggering** despite correct configurations
■ **API-related errors** when integrating Smartsheet with other platforms
■ **Performance issues** with large datasets or complex workflows
■ **Permissions and access problems** in shared workspaces
■ **Subscription or billing issues**

For **general troubleshooting**, consider checking the **Smartsheet Knowledge Base or Community Forum** first. If those don't resolve your issue, contacting Smartsheet Support is the next step.

2. Smartsheet Support Options

Smartsheet offers multiple levels of support, depending on your **subscription plan** and the urgency of your issue.

◆ **Self-Service Support Options (Available to All Users)**

📍 **Smartsheet Help Center** (https://help.smartsheet.com)
🔍 **Best for:** General troubleshooting, automation guides, workflow documentation.

📍 **Smartsheet Community Forum** (https://community.smartsheet.com)
🔍 **Best for:** Peer-to-peer support, common issue resolutions, and best practices.

📍 **Smartsheet Status Page** (https://status.smartsheet.com)
🔍 **Best for:** Checking if there's a **system-wide issue** causing disruptions.

◆ **Direct Support Options**

☐ **Live Chat Support**

📍 Available at: https://www.smartsheet.com/contact
🔍 **Best for:** Quick answers to basic issues, automation guidance, minor troubleshooting.

☐ **Email Support**

📍 Available at: https://help.smartsheet.com/contact
🔍 **Best for:** Complex automation errors, workflow failures, API integration problems.

⬛ **Pro Tip:** Include **screenshots, error messages, and a description of your workflow** to speed up the resolution.

3️⃣ **Phone Support (For Enterprise & Business Plan Users)**

📍 Available via Smartsheet's Enterprise Support Team.
🔍 **Best for: Urgent automation failures** affecting business operations.

4️⃣ **Smartsheet Professional Services**

📍 Available for **custom consulting and workflow optimization**.
🔍 **Best for: Custom automation setups, advanced API integrations, and workflow audits**.

💡 **Note:** This is a paid service designed for businesses looking for hands-on assistance.

---

3. How to Submit an Effective Support Ticket

To **get faster and more accurate help**, include the following details when submitting a support request:

⬛ **Problem Summary:** Clearly explain what's not working.
⬛ **Steps Taken:** List the troubleshooting steps you've already tried.
⬛ **Error Messages:** Include screenshots or exact wording of error messages.
⬛ **Automation Details:** Describe how your workflow is set up and what outcome you expected.
⬛ **Account Type:** Mention whether you are on a **Free, Business, or Enterprise plan** (some features are plan-specific).

---

4. What to Expect After Submitting a Request

📌 **Response Time:**

- **Free & Pro users:** Expect a response within **24-48 hours**.
- **Business & Enterprise users:** Typically get priority responses within **a few hours**.
- **Phone Support:** Immediate assistance (for Enterprise users).

📌 **Follow-Up Steps:**

- **Check your email** for updates from the support team.
- **Provide any additional details** if requested.
- **Test suggested solutions** and report back if the issue persists.

⬛ **Pro Tip:** If you don't get a response within the expected timeframe, follow up using **Live Chat** for quicker escalation.

Conclusion

Smartsheet offers **multiple support options** to assist users in troubleshooting complex automation issues. By **using the appropriate support channel and providing detailed information**, you can ensure **a faster and more effective resolution**.

Section 8:
The Future of Automation in Smartsheet

Preparing for AI-Driven Automation Trends

Artificial Intelligence (AI) is transforming the way businesses operate, and **Smartsheet is no exception**. AI-driven automation is poised to **revolutionize workflows**, making them **more efficient, intelligent, and predictive**.

In this chapter, we will explore:
- **The impact of AI on automation**
- **How AI-driven automation will enhance Smartsheet workflows**
- **Steps to prepare for AI advancements in Smartsheet**

---

1. The Role of AI in Automation

AI is advancing automation by **reducing manual intervention**, improving decision-making, and **predicting outcomes** based on past data. Smartsheet and other **work management platforms** are incorporating AI to:

📌 **Enhance workflow intelligence** – AI can suggest **automation rules** based on past behaviors.
📌 **Optimize task assignments** – AI-driven automation can allocate tasks based on **employee workload and efficiency**.
📌 **Predict workflow bottlenecks** – AI can analyze patterns and **forecast delays in projects**.
📌 **Improve data accuracy** – AI-powered tools help **validate inputs, detect anomalies, and prevent errors**.

With AI, **Smartsheet users can expect more sophisticated automation capabilities** that go beyond **basic rule-based workflows**.

---

2. How AI-Driven Automation Will Transform Smartsheet

🚀 Future AI enhancements in Smartsheet could include:

- **1. AI-Powered Workflow Optimization**

  - Smartsheet may introduce AI-driven **workflow recommendations** based on project structures and **historical data**.
  - AI will suggest **optimizations** to reduce **bottlenecks and inefficiencies**.

- **2. Predictive Task Management**

  - AI will analyze team performance and **predict which tasks may cause delays**.
  - AI-generated **priority lists** will help managers **reallocate resources efficiently**.

- **3. Smart Data Processing & Insights**

  - AI will **automatically categorize and analyze data** for reports.

- AI-driven insights will **detect trends and suggest next actions** based on historical performance.

◆ **4. Automated Decision-Making in Workflows**

- AI could **automate approval processes** based on set parameters.
- AI-driven logic will allow workflows to **adapt dynamically** to changing project conditions.

◆ **5. AI Chatbots for Smartsheet Assistance**

- AI-powered virtual assistants will help users **set up automation rules** quickly.
- Chatbots could **respond to queries, troubleshoot issues, and provide real-time guidance**.

---

3. Preparing for AI-Driven Automation in Smartsheet

As AI becomes more integrated into Smartsheet, it's crucial to **adapt and prepare**. Here's how:

1. Stay Updated with Smartsheet AI Enhancements

- Follow **Smartsheet updates and webinars** on AI-driven automation.
- Join the **Smartsheet Community** to discuss AI-powered features with other users.

2. Learn AI & Machine Learning Basics

- Gain a basic understanding of **how AI works** in business automation.
- Explore **AI-driven project management tools** and case studies.

3. Implement Data-Driven Automation Now

- Start using **Smartsheet's advanced formulas** to get comfortable with data-driven decisions.
- Experiment with **conditional logic, workflow triggers, and automation sequencing**.

4. Prepare for AI-Enhanced Reporting & Analysis

- Ensure your Smartsheet data is **well-structured and accurate**—AI works best with **clean, organized data**.
- Begin integrating **business intelligence tools** (such as Power BI or Tableau) with Smartsheet for deeper insights.

5. Experiment with AI-Powered Integrations

- Smartsheet may expand its AI capabilities by **integrating with AI-powered tools like Zapier, Power Automate, and Google AI**.
- Start testing AI-enhanced integrations **to automate data collection, analysis, and decision-making**.

Conclusion

AI-driven automation is **the future of Smartsheet workflows**. By leveraging AI, businesses will experience **smarter task management, predictive analytics, and optimized workflows**.

To stay ahead, **embrace AI advancements early, optimize your Smartsheet automations, and build a data-driven workflow strategy**.

Continuous Learning and Skill Development

The world of automation is **constantly evolving**, and Smartsheet is no exception. To **stay ahead of the curve**, professionals need to embrace **continuous learning and skill development**.

In this chapter, we will explore:
■ **Why continuous learning is essential for automation professionals**
■ **Key learning resources for mastering Smartsheet automation**
■ **Strategies to develop expertise and stay updated on automation trends**

---

1. The Importance of Continuous Learning in Automation

Automation is an **ever-changing field** with frequent updates, new integrations, and **AI-driven enhancements**. Continuous learning ensures that you:

📌 **Keep up with Smartsheet updates** – Smartsheet regularly introduces **new automation features and integrations**.
📌 **Stay competitive in your industry** – Employers **prioritize professionals** who continuously **adapt and learn**.
📌 **Maximize automation capabilities** – Learning new automation techniques helps **eliminate inefficiencies** and improve workflows.
📌 **Prepare for AI-driven automation trends** – As AI becomes more integrated into **workflow management**, staying informed will help you **leverage AI tools effectively**.

---

2. Essential Learning Resources for Smartsheet Automation

🚀 **To develop Smartsheet automation expertise, leverage the following resources:**

• **1. Smartsheet Learning Center**

📍 **Smartsheet Help & Learning Center** ([Smartsheet Help] (https://help.smartsheet.com/)) provides official tutorials, guides, and FAQs.
📍 **Automation-specific learning modules** help users understand Smartsheet's **workflow capabilities**.

• **2. Smartsheet University**

📍 **Smartsheet University** offers structured courses and certifications for beginners and advanced users.
📍 It includes **self-paced training and instructor-led courses** on automation.

• **3. Smartsheet Community & Forums**

📍 Join the **Smartsheet Community Forum** ([community.smartsheet.com] (https://community.smartsheet.com/)) to ask questions and share experiences.
📍 Participate in discussions to **discover best practices and innovative automation strategies**.

• **4. Webinars, Blogs, and YouTube Tutorials**

📍 Smartsheet frequently hosts **webinars** on advanced automation techniques.
📍 Follow **Smartsheet's official blog** for feature updates and case studies.
📍 Explore **YouTube tutorials** from automation experts for step-by-step guides.

• **5. Online Courses & Certifications**

📍 Websites like **Udemy, Coursera, and LinkedIn Learning** offer courses on **automation, project management, and Smartsheet workflows**.

📍 Pursuing certifications **enhances credibility** and helps you stay updated on best practices.

- **6. Networking with Automation Experts**

📍 Join LinkedIn groups and professional communities to **connect with Smartsheet experts**.

📍 Attend automation-focused **conferences and virtual summits**.

---

3. Developing Expertise in Smartsheet Automation

📌 To **become proficient in Smartsheet automation**, focus on:

1. Hands-On Practice

- Experiment with **different automation workflows** in Smartsheet.
- Use **trial-and-error methods** to understand how automation works in real-world scenarios.

2. Mastering Advanced Automation Features

- Learn how to **combine multiple automation tools** for **complex workflows**.
- Explore **formulas, conditional logic, and integrations** with third-party tools like **Zapier and Power Automate**.

3. Staying Updated with New Smartsheet Features

- Follow **Smartsheet's product updates and roadmap** to adapt to new automation enhancements.
- Regularly review Smartsheet's **release notes** to learn about **improvements and new automation capabilities**.

4. Experimenting with AI-Driven Automation

- Explore AI-powered workflow suggestions as Smartsheet integrates **AI-driven automation tools**.
- Test AI-based integrations with **machine learning-powered automation**.

5. Building a Knowledge-Sharing Culture

- Share automation best practices **within your team or organization**.
- Train colleagues on **how to implement automation efficiently** to improve overall productivity.

Conclusion

Continuous learning is **the key to maximizing Smartsheet automation**. By staying updated on **new features, mastering advanced techniques, and leveraging AI-powered automation trends**, you can remain **at the forefront of workflow efficiency**.

Recap of Key Automation Strategies

Throughout this book, we have explored the **full spectrum of Smartsheet automation**, from **basic workflow automations** to **advanced AI-driven strategies**. This final chapter serves as a **recap of the most critical automation techniques** that can **enhance efficiency, eliminate manual tasks, and optimize business processes**.

By revisiting these key strategies, you will have a **comprehensive understanding** of how to implement **effective automation workflows** in Smartsheet.

---

1. Foundational Automation Strategies

■ Understanding Automation & Its Role in Modern Workflows

* Automation eliminates **repetitive manual tasks**, reducing **human error** and increasing **productivity**.
* Smartsheet provides **rule-based automation workflows**, allowing **teams to streamline approvals, reminders, and notifications**.

■ Setting Up Your Smartsheet Account for Automation

* Ensure that your **Smartsheet account** is configured properly with **appropriate permissions** to enable automation.
* Define **automation permissions and roles** to control **who can create, modify, and manage workflows**.

■ Core Smartsheet Automation Features

* **Alerts & Reminders**: Automatically notify **team members** about **deadlines, status updates, or pending tasks**.
* **Recurring Tasks & Approvals**: Schedule **repetitive tasks** and automate **approval workflows** to save time.
* **Task Assignments & Notifications**: Automatically assign tasks based on **trigger conditions** and notify users.
* **Workflow Automation for Project Management**: Use automated workflows to **track progress, escalate issues, and ensure alignment**.
* **Data Capture with Forms**: Use Smartsheet **forms** to automate data collection and integrate responses into workflows.
* **Scheduled Summaries & Reports**: Automate the delivery of **summary reports** to key stakeholders on a regular basis.

---

2. Advanced Automation Techniques

■ Combining Multiple Automation Tools

* Leverage **layered automation workflows** by integrating **multiple rules** for complex business scenarios.

■ Leveraging Formulas for Dynamic Automation

* Use Smartsheet formulas such as **IF, COUNTIF, INDEX/MATCH, and VLOOKUP** to **automatically trigger actions** within your sheets.

■ Implementing Conditional Logic in Automations

* Utilize **if-then logic** to create **smart workflows** that adjust dynamically based on **changing conditions**.

■ Integrating Smartsheet with External Applications

* Use **Zapier, Power Automate, or APIs** to connect Smartsheet with **other business applications**, such as:

  * **Microsoft Teams & Slack** for real-time communication
  * **CRM systems** (Salesforce, HubSpot) for **automated lead management**
  * **Finance tools** (QuickBooks, Xero) for **budget tracking**

■ Using Smartsheet API for Custom Automation

* Implement **custom integrations and scripts** using the **Smartsheet API** to extend automation capabilities beyond built-in features.

---

3. Real-World Use Cases for Automation

📌 Project Management Automation

* Automate **task tracking, milestone updates, and resource allocation** to keep projects on schedule.

📌 Marketing Automation

* Schedule automated **campaign tracking, email reminders, and social media posts** for marketing teams.

📌 HR Process Optimization

* Use **Smartsheet workflows to streamline employee onboarding, leave requests, and performance reviews**.

📌 Manufacturing & Operations Automation

* Implement **inventory tracking, quality control alerts, and automated compliance reporting**.

📌 Financial & Budget Tracking

* Automate **monthly financial reports, budget approvals, and expense tracking workflows**.

📌 Customer Service & Ticketing Automation

* Improve customer experience with **automated support ticket escalation, status updates, and resolution tracking**.

---

4. Best Practices for Scaling Automation

■ 1. Start Simple & Build Gradually

* Begin with **basic automations** before implementing **complex workflow combinations**.

■ 2. Regularly Review & Optimize Workflows

- Evaluate **automation performance** using **productivity metrics** and adjust rules as needed.

■ 3. Ensure Data Security & Compliance

- Maintain **user permissions** and access controls to **protect sensitive data**.

■ 4. Encourage Continuous Learning

- Stay updated on **Smartsheet's new automation features** and **emerging AI-driven automation trends**.

Conclusion

Automation is not just a **one-time implementation**—it is a **continuous improvement process**. By mastering **Smartsheet automation strategies**, you can **significantly reduce manual work, increase efficiency**, and **boost team productivity**.

🚀 With the right automation mindset, you can future-proof your workflow strategies and fully harness the power of Smartsheet automation!

Appendices

Appendix A: Smartsheet Automation Templates and Checklists

To help you **implement Smartsheet automation efficiently**, this appendix provides a collection of **pre-built templates and checklists** for **various automation scenarios**. These templates can be **customized** to fit your workflow and help you quickly **set up automated processes** with minimal effort.

1. Smartsheet Automation Templates

Below are **ready-to-use automation templates** that can be imported into Smartsheet to **simplify** your automation setup.

■ Project Management Automation Template

* Automatically assigns tasks based on status updates
* Sends alerts when deadlines are approaching
* Tracks project progress with automated reports

■ Task Assignment & Notification Template

* Assigns new tasks to team members based on workload
* Sends automatic email and in-app notifications
* Tracks task completion and escalates overdue tasks

■ Recurring Task & Approval Workflow Template

* Creates **weekly or monthly** task reminders
* Automates multi-level **approval workflows**
* Notifies stakeholders once approvals are completed

■ HR Onboarding Automation Template

* Sends **automated emails** to new employees with onboarding checklists
* Assigns onboarding tasks to HR team members
* Tracks document submissions and training progress

■ Marketing Campaign Automation Template

* Automates email sequences for marketing campaigns
* Tracks campaign performance using **automated reports**
* Schedules **social media posts** based on predefined triggers

■ Customer Support Ticketing Automation Template

* Creates a **ticket tracking system** for incoming support requests
* Notifies **support agents** when tickets are assigned
* Escalates unresolved tickets based on priority

■ Financial & Budget Tracking Template

* Tracks **monthly expenses and revenue**
* Generates **automated financial reports**
* Sends alerts for **budget overruns or financial risks**

---

2. Smartsheet Automation Setup Checklists

Use these **checklists** to ensure that your **automation workflows** are set up correctly and optimized for performance.

🔍 General Automation Setup Checklist

✔ Clearly define **workflow objectives** before setting up automation
✔ Identify **key triggers** (date-based, status change, form submissions, etc.)
✔ Assign **automation permissions** to the right team members
✔ Test automation workflows in a **sandbox environment** before deploying
✔ Monitor **workflow performance and error logs**

🔍 Project Management Automation Checklist

✔ Create a **project tracking sheet** with key milestones
✔ Set up **automated reminders** for approaching deadlines
✔ Automate **task assignments** based on project phase
✔ Generate **weekly status reports** automatically

🔍 Task Assignment & Notifications Checklist

✔ Define **task categories and owners**
✔ Set up **automated alerts** for task updates
✔ Enable **escalation workflows** for overdue tasks
✔ Ensure **notifications are sent via email and Smartsheet mobile app**

🔍 HR Onboarding Checklist

✔ Automate the **onboarding checklist** for new employees
✔ Assign onboarding tasks to **HR personnel**
✔ Enable document submission tracking
✔ Schedule **training reminders** for new hires

🔍 Marketing Campaign Automation Checklist

✔ Set up an **automated email sequence** for leads
✔ Automate **ad performance tracking and reporting**
✔ Schedule **social media posts and engagement tracking**
✔ Generate **weekly marketing reports**

🔍 Customer Service Automation Checklist

✔ Create a **support ticketing system**
✔ Automate **ticket escalation workflows** for high-priority cases
✔ Send **status updates** to customers automatically
✔ Track **average resolution time** for performance insights

🔍 Finance & Budget Tracking Checklist

✔ Automate **expense reporting and approvals**
✔ Set up **budget alerts** for cost overruns
✔ Generate **monthly financial summaries**
✔ Enable **automated invoice tracking**

---

3. How to Use These Templates & Checklists

📌 Step 1: Download the Template

Smartsheet provides **pre-built automation templates** that can be customized for your workflow.

📌 Step 2: Customize Based on Your Needs

Modify automation **rules, triggers, and notifications** to match your business requirements.

📌 Step 3: Test and Optimize

Run a **test workflow** to ensure that all automations function as expected.

📌 Step 4: Monitor & Adjust

Regularly review **automation logs** to ensure that workflows remain **efficient and error-free**.

Using **Smartsheet automation templates and checklists** can significantly **accelerate implementation** and **reduce errors** in automation workflows. By leveraging these **pre-built frameworks**, you can **streamline your processes, boost efficiency, and optimize automation for long-term success.**

Appendix B: Glossary of Key Automation Terms

Understanding **automation terminology** is essential for maximizing your use of **Smartsheet automation**. This glossary provides **clear definitions** of key automation-related terms used throughout this book, helping you to **grasp fundamental concepts** and apply them effectively.

A

Action

An **automated response** triggered by a **specific condition** in a workflow. Examples include **sending an alert, assigning a task, or updating a record**.

Alert

A **notification** (via email, Smartsheet app, or Slack) that informs users about **important changes** or updates in a sheet.

API (Application Programming Interface)

A set of **rules and protocols** that allows different applications to **communicate with Smartsheet** for **custom automation and integrations**.

B

Bot

An **automated script or tool** that performs **repetitive tasks** without manual intervention, often used in workflow automation.

Business Rules

Predefined **conditions and logic** that dictate how an automation should behave based on **specific triggers and conditions**.

C

Conditional Logic

Rules that **modify automation behavior** based on **IF-THEN conditions**. For example, sending different alerts **based on task priority**.

Connector

A **pre-built integration tool** that allows Smartsheet to **connect with external applications** like **Microsoft Teams, Slack, or Zapier**.

Custom Workflow

A **user-defined automation** in Smartsheet, allowing teams to **automate processes** without coding.

D

Data Mapping

The process of **aligning data fields** between Smartsheet and other systems when using **integrations or APIs**.

Dynamic Dropdown

A **dropdown list** that updates automatically based on **linked cell values** or **form inputs**.

E

Escalation Rule

A **workflow rule** that triggers an action **if a task remains incomplete** beyond a set deadline.

Event-Based Trigger

An **automation trigger** that activates based on **user actions** (e.g., when a new row is added).

F

Form Automation

The process of **automatically capturing data** from a Smartsheet **form submission** and triggering workflows based on the input.

Formula-Based Automation

Using **Smartsheet formulas** to trigger automated actions, such as updating statuses or calculating progress.

G

Gantt Chart Automation

The use of **automated rules** to update **task dependencies and timelines** within Smartsheet's Gantt Chart view.

Governance Rules

Security and compliance rules that **restrict access, automation permissions, and data usage**.

I

Integration

The ability to **connect Smartsheet with third-party apps** like Google Drive, Salesforce, and Slack to **automate workflows across multiple platforms**.

L

Lookup Function

A formula-based function used in **automation workflows** to **pull data from related sheets** dynamically.

Low-Code Automation

A **drag-and-drop or rule-based** automation setup that does not require advanced coding skills.

M

Macros

A set of **predefined automation steps** that **execute multiple actions** simultaneously in a workflow.

Multi-Step Automation

An **automation workflow** that includes **sequential actions**, such as **sending an alert, updating a row, and triggering another action**.

N

Notification

An **automated alert** (via email, in-app, or push notifications) that informs users of **workflow changes** or **task updates**.

O

Object-Based Automation

Automation based on **Smartsheet objects** (rows, columns, or cells) to **apply conditional formatting or calculations dynamically**.

On-Demand Automation

An automation that runs **only when manually triggered** by a user.

P

Permissions-Based Automation

Workflows that execute **only for specific user roles**, such as **admins approving requests** while **team members submit requests**.

Pre-Built Workflow

An **automation template** that can be **imported and customized** in Smartsheet.

R

Recurring Automation

An **automated process** that runs on **a set schedule** (daily, weekly, or monthly).

Role-Based Access Control (RBAC)

A security feature that restricts **automation actions** based on **user roles and permissions**.

S

Scheduled Automation

Workflows that run at **specific times or intervals**, such as **weekly reporting summaries**.

Smart Column

A column that updates automatically **based on automation rules** (e.g., status changes dynamically when tasks are marked complete).

System-Generated Alert

An **automatic notification** triggered by **Smartsheet backend rules**, such as **workflow failures or missing data warnings**.

T

Task Dependency Automation

An automation that **adjusts task timelines** based on **preceding tasks** in a project plan.

Trigger

An event that **initiates an automation**, such as **adding a row, changing a status, or reaching a due date**.

U

User-Defined Workflow

A custom automation that follows **manually configured conditions and actions**.

V

Validation Rule

A rule that **ensures data integrity** before automation actions are executed (e.g., preventing empty submissions).

Version Control Automation

An automation that **tracks changes** and **stores version history** in Smartsheet.

W

Workflow

A sequence of **automated steps** that process data, trigger actions, and execute Smartsheet functions.

Webhooks

A Smartsheet **API feature** that allows real-time **data synchronization** with external applications.

Z

Zapier Integration

A tool that allows Smartsheet to **connect with thousands of other applications** for extended automation capabilities.

This glossary provides **key automation-related terms** essential for **working efficiently** with Smartsheet. Understanding these terms will help you **navigate automation workflows, optimize processes, and troubleshoot errors** effectively.

🚀 **Use this glossary as a reference whenever you encounter new automation concepts in Smartsheet!**

Appendix C: Additional Resources and Learning Tools

Automation in Smartsheet is constantly evolving, and staying up to date with **new features, best practices, and expert tips** will help you maximize efficiency. This appendix provides a list of **additional resources and learning tools** to help you **expand your knowledge, troubleshoot challenges, and refine your automation skills**.

1. Official Smartsheet Resources

Smartsheet Learning Center

- **Website:** [Smartsheet Learning Center] (https://help.smartsheet.com/)
- **Description:** The **official learning portal** for Smartsheet, featuring **training videos, tutorials, and best practices** for automation workflows.

Smartsheet Help & Support

- **Website:** [Smartsheet Help Center] (https://help.smartsheet.com/)
- **Description:** Access to **comprehensive documentation** on Smartsheet's features, including step-by-step guides for automation.

Smartsheet Community Forum

- **Website:** [Smartsheet Community] (https://community.smartsheet.com/)
- **Description:** A forum where users can **ask questions, share best practices, and get insights** from experienced Smartsheet professionals.

Smartsheet API Documentation

- **Website:** [Smartsheet API Docs] (https://smartsheet.redoc.ly/)
- **Description:** The official API documentation, including **code examples, integration guides, and API reference materials** for developers.

2. Smartsheet Training and Certification

Smartsheet University

- **Website:** [Smartsheet University] (https://smartu.smartsheet.com/)
- **Description:** Offers **self-paced courses, instructor-led training, and certifications** to help you **become an expert in automation**.

Smartsheet Certified Professional Exam

- **Website:** [Smartsheet Certification] (https://smartsheet.com/certification)
- **Description:** Earn a **Smartsheet certification** to validate your skills in **workflow automation, reporting, and project management**.

3. Online Courses and Tutorials

LinkedIn Learning – Smartsheet Courses

- **Website:** [LinkedIn Learning] (https://www.linkedin.com/learning/)
- **Description:** Professional Smartsheet courses covering **automation workflows, integrations, and best practices**.

Udemy – Smartsheet Training

- **Website:** [Udemy] (https://www.udemy.com/)
- **Description:** Comprehensive, **affordable courses** on using Smartsheet for **automation, project management, and collaboration**.

YouTube – Smartsheet Tutorials

- **Website:** [YouTube] (https://www.youtube.com/)
- **Channels to Follow:**
  - **Smartsheet Official Channel** – Covers **feature updates, automation guides, and expert insights**.
  - **Technology Trainers** – Provides **step-by-step automation tutorials** for all skill levels.
  - **Productivity Guru** – Focuses on **real-world Smartsheet automation applications**.

---

4. Smartsheet Integrations & Automation Tools

Zapier

- **Website:** [Zapier Smartsheet Integration] (https://zapier.com/apps/smartsheet/integrations)
- **Description:** Connects Smartsheet with **thousands of apps** (e.g., Slack, Trello, Google Sheets) to create **automated workflows**.

Power Automate (Microsoft)

- **Website:** [Power Automate] (https://powerautomate.microsoft.com/)
- **Description:** A tool that **automates Smartsheet actions** with **Microsoft apps** like Teams, Outlook, and Excel.

Make (formerly Integromat)

- **Website:** [Make.com] (https://www.make.com/)
- **Description:** Provides **advanced workflow automation** capabilities for integrating Smartsheet with **other business applications**.

Smartsheet Connectors

- **Website:** [Smartsheet Connectors] (https://www.smartsheet.com/platform/connectors)
- **Description:** Official integrations for **Salesforce, Jira, Microsoft Dynamics, and more** to automate enterprise workflows.

---

5. Books & Guides on Automation & Smartsheet

Books on Smartsheet & Workflow Automation

1. **"Mastering Smartsheet: Building Efficient Workflows for Business Success"**
   - Covers **Smartsheet automation, dashboards, and collaboration features**.
2. **"The Smartsheet User Guide: From Basics to Advanced Techniques"**
   - Walks through **automation, formulas, and integrations**.
3. **"Workflow Automation for Beginners: Optimize Your Business Processes with No-Code Tools"**
   - Discusses **Smartsheet, Zapier, Power Automate, and other automation tools**.

Industry-Specific Guides

- **"Project Management with Smartsheet: Best Practices for Agile & Waterfall Teams"**
- **"Marketing Automation with Smartsheet: Streamlining Campaigns & Reporting"**
- **"Smartsheet for Finance: Automating Budgeting & Expense Tracking"**

---

6. Expert Communities & Blogs

Reddit – Smartsheet Community

- **Website:** [r/Smartsheet] (https://www.reddit.com/r/Smartsheet/)
- **Description:** Discussions on **automation use cases, troubleshooting, and feature requests**.

Smartsheet Blog

- **Website:** [Smartsheet Blog] (https://www.smartsheet.com/blog)
- **Description:** News, case studies, and automation best practices from Smartsheet experts.

Smartsheet Champions Program

- **Website:** [Smartsheet Champions] (https://www.smartsheet.com/champions)
- **Description:** A program for **power users** to **get exclusive training, share insights, and participate in product feedback**.

---

7. AI & Future Trends in Automation

Artificial Intelligence & Automation Trends

- **Smartsheet AI Features Overview** → Learn how **AI is shaping automation in Smartsheet**.
- **AI-Powered Workflow Optimization** → Automate **data analysis, approvals, and task prioritization** using AI.
- **AI & Machine Learning in Business Automation** → Explore **next-gen automation trends**.

Whether you're a **beginner learning Smartsheet automation** or an **advanced user looking to optimize complex workflows**, these resources will help you **stay updated, troubleshoot effectively, and develop advanced automation skills**.

🚀 Use these resources to enhance your Smartsheet automation expertise and streamline your workflows!

Conclusion

Throughout this book, we have explored the vast capabilities of **Smartsheet automation** and how it can **transform workflows, increase efficiency, and reduce manual tasks**. By leveraging Smartsheet's **automation tools, integrations, and best practices**, you now have the knowledge to optimize **project management, reporting, HR processes, marketing campaigns, financial tracking, and more**.

Automation is no longer just a convenience—it is a **necessity** for businesses and teams that strive for **scalability, productivity, and competitive advantage**. By using Smartsheet's built-in **workflows, formulas, notifications, and integrations**, you can **automate repetitive tasks, standardize processes, and improve collaboration** across departments.

Key Takeaways

As we close this guide, let's revisit some of the **key takeaways** from this book:

- **Understanding Automation's Role** → Automation **reduces manual effort**, minimizes errors, and increases team productivity.
- **Setting Up a Strong Foundation** → A well-configured **Smartsheet account with proper permissions** ensures secure and efficient automation.
- **Leveraging Core Automation Features** → **Alerts, reminders, task assignments, and workflow automation** streamline operations.
- **Exploring Advanced Techniques** → **Conditional logic, API integration, and multi-tool automation** create highly efficient and complex workflows.
- **Applying Automation to Real-World Scenarios** → Automation enhances **project management, marketing, HR, finance, and customer service**.
- **Adopting Best Practices** → Efficient automation **design, security compliance, and performance measurement** ensure long-term success.
- **Continuous Learning and Adaptation** → The automation landscape is evolving with **AI, machine learning, and new Smartsheet features**.

By mastering these **principles and techniques**, you are well-equipped to **build powerful automation workflows that drive productivity and operational excellence**.

Your Next Steps

Now that you have a solid foundation in **Smartsheet automation**, the next step is **to apply what you've learned to real-world scenarios**. Here are a few **actionable steps** you can take:

1. **Start Small** – Automate simple processes such as **task notifications, approval workflows, or report generation** before scaling up.
2. **Experiment & Optimize** – Test different **workflows, conditional logic, and integrations** to find what works best for your organization.
3. **Explore New Features** – Stay updated with **Smartsheet's latest automation tools, AI enhancements, and third-party integrations**.
4. **Engage with the Community** – Join the **Smartsheet Community, attend webinars, and participate in discussions** to learn from experts.
5. **Measure & Improve** – Track automation success through **KPIs, performance reports, and team feedback** to refine your workflows.

Automation is a **journey, not a one-time setup**. As your team grows and your processes evolve, **continue refining and expanding your automation strategies**.

Final Thoughts

Smartsheet is an incredibly **powerful and versatile** platform that enables users to **build intelligent workflows, integrate with external tools, and leverage AI-driven automation**. Whether you're **managing projects, streamlining business processes, or enhancing team collaboration**, automation is the key to unlocking **greater efficiency and success**.

By embracing **continuous learning and innovation**, you will be **at the forefront of automation-driven productivity** in your organization. **The future of work is automated, and with Smartsheet, you are ready to lead that transformation**.

🚀 **Now, go forth and automate with confidence!** 🚀

www.ingramcontent.com/pod-product-compliance
Lightning Source LLC
LaVergne TN
LVHW081758050326
832903LV00027B/2000